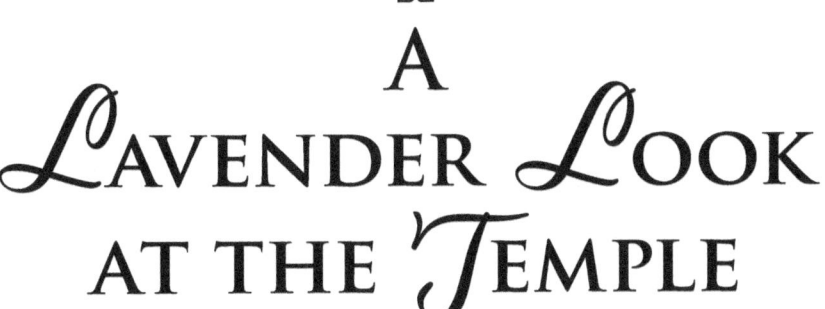

A LAVENDER LOOK AT THE TEMPLE

A Gay Perspective of the Peoples Temple

Michael Bellefountaine
with Dora Bellefountaine

iUniverse, Inc.
Bloomington

A Lavender Look at the Temple
A Gay Perspective of the Peoples Temple

iUniverse books may be ordered through booksellers or by contacting:

iUniverse
1663 Liberty Drive
Bloomington, IN 47403
www.iuniverse.com
1-800-Authors (1-800-288-4677)

ISBN: 978-1-4620-3529-8 (sc)
ISBN: 978-1-4620-3527-4 (hc)
ISBN: 978-1-4620-3528-1 (e)

Printed in the United States of America

iUniverse rev. date: 8/3/2011

"It is easy to become obsessed with the deaths, with the final moments of Jonestown. The melodrama of the suicides swallows up Jim Jones and the Peoples Temple. But Jonestown represents more than nine hundred bodies.

They, in fact, obscure the real issues.

For Peoples Temple as it lived is of much greater significance than Peoples Temple as it died. Even then we must penetrate beyond Peoples Temple as such.

We must go in search of the ideas it claimed to embody."

Shiva Naipaul

Dedication and Author's Thanks

This book is dedicated to Peoples Temple, especially its gay and lesbian members, specifically Monica Bagby, Edith Cordell, Loretta Stewart Cordell Coomer, Vernon Gosney, Pat Grunnet, Garry Lambrev, Linda Mills, Tobi Stone, Teresa king, Diane Lundquist, T. Keith Wade, Deanna Wilkinson.

Special thanks to my mother, Dora, my dad, Ronnie, all of my brothers and sisters, especially Cathy, as well as my nieces, nephews and my father Reggie Dalessandro.

To the ACTUP/SF collective and membership whose support made this project a reality. Specifically Adrian, Aiko, Andrea, Banka, Benjamin, Betty, David, Derek, Erin, Edward, Frank, Jerry, Jessie, Josh, Kyle, Lauren, Maynard, Michael M., Mickey, Mira, Nadia, Patrick, Petey, Ruthie, Sistar, Susan, Steve, Stacy, Tate, Todd, Travis and Karl Goldman.

Professor Dolinger at San Francisco State University Jewish classes listening and encouraging me with my project. Professor Dolinger became a very close friend.

Thanks to Fielding McGehee for endless hours editing and Professor Rebecca Moore helping with the research from the Jonestown Institute at www.jonestown.sdsu.edu

Also to Laura Kohl (a Jonestown survivor) who became a dear friend.

The help I received from the staff at California Historical Society and the San Francisco Public Library was invaluable. From the CHS I was able to retrieve records of Peoples Temple and from SFPL I was able to get records on Harvey Milk.

CONTENTS

$\mathcal{F}$OREWORD

by Erin Evans

"Any fool can make history, but it takes a genius to write it."
Oscar Wilde

"History is always written wrong, and so always needs to be rewritten."
George Santayana

The story of the Peoples Temple is widely known because of a tragic event that encompassed only a snippet of the organization's history. Their story exploded through a highly sensationalized lens, and that story continues to be told and retold through that limited lens. The Temple's history remained comprised of those relative short moments of tragedy, despite twenty years of Temple activity from which storytellers could have drawn.

Michael Bellefountaine saw beyond that limited lens and pursued a unique and important perspective of the Temple – the lavender perspective. In the process of conducting exhaustive interviews with former Temple members, including many whom had never before come forward, and delving through archives Michael assembled a mosaic-like story of the Lesbian, Gay, Bisexual and Transgender experience in the Temple. His work also illuminated a most central tenet in research that is too often neglected. Conscious relativism in academic and journalistic research is integral to manufacturing accurate and socially just narratives in historical research. By relativism I mean what Michael so eloquently wrote about in his article for the Jonestown Review in 2004.

During his research on the LGBT community with in the Temple Michael was confronted with major factual differences in survivors' accounts of life in Jonestown. He explained how he dealt with these differences in his article

"In Search of Truth", and his explanation captures the concept of conscious relativism.

> The difference in accounts depends upon the perspective of the speaker, the circumstance of their presence in Jonestown, their relationship with Jim Jones and other members, and their journey in the intervening 26 years. Even through we can verify and justify any number of the arguments, it is true that some people's account of events differ and often times can be directly contradictory. That seems to be how human nature and history work. Instead of using one to negate the other, we have to record the difference. Many times an historian can reconstruct what has happened through the various accounts, understanding that they all differ ... We need to focus every effort to record all of the feelings, stories and remembrances of Jonestown community – even when they seem to disagree – before they are lost in time. (The Jonestown Report, October 2004, Volume 6)

The assertion to "record the difference" reflects relativism in research. And the focus on first hand accounts storytelling is the route to that record. This book is Dora Bellefountaine's effort to not only make her son's valuable research known, but to also add to the record of Michael's valuable life story. As an activist and researcher Michael put his entire self into his work; this book rests upon countless hours of interviewing, transcribing, sifting through archival records, reading, etc.

Exposing the truth was Michael's life passion, and he was relentless in it. In his life choices and even in the small details of each day Michael acted on an ethic of blunt and unrestricted honesty. Michael's portfolio of civil disobedience in the name of exposing the truth and empowering marginalized communities reflects his commitment of unmasking those in power. In the Temple's case the mask was comprised of a highly sensationalized narrative that completely demonized Jim Jones and his organization. In power are those few who have manufactured Jonestown's story with the limited lens of tragedy and villains. A Lavender Look at the Peoples Temple is not a political work. Rather, it is one piece of the mosaic that is the Peoples Temple, told through a unique and important lens.

$\mathcal{P}$REFACE

by Dora Bellefountaine

My son, Michael, was born March 28, 1966. He grew up in rural Maine, and graduated from Gorham High School class of 1984. He attended the University of Southern Maine where he discovered his talent and calling as an activist organizer of Lesbian, Gay, Bisexual and Transgender rights.

In 1989 he got involved with ACTUP and co-founded the Maine Chapter. Michael moved to Florida in 1990 and joined ACTUP in Sarasota and Tampa. There he met fellow activist and best friend, David Paquarilli. Both Michael and David decided to move to San Francisco. In San Francisco, along with Todd Swindell, Ronnie Burk and other dedicated activists enlightened to inherent problems with AIDS paradigm, they founded ACTUP San Francisco. ACTUP/SF protested against AIDS Service Organizations who irresponsibly used scarce funding for AIDS patients, and against the pharmaceutical industry that profited from people scared into taking toxic AIDS drugs with questionable efficacy. Wanting to do more for people suffering with AIDS, ACTUP/SF opened a collectively-owned medical marijuana dispensary on Market Street, where they could simultaneously protest federal law against this medicine, and subsidize their strife for AIDS reform. From 1998-2004 Michael worked full-time as an activist.

Pursuing his lifelong love of history, Michael enrolled at San Francisco State University in 2004. He quickly focused on the historical connection between Jim Jones' Peoples Temple and the city of San Francisco, and the relationship that Harvey Milk, San Francisco's gay councilman, had with Peoples Temple. Michael's interest in primary source materials on the temple led him to contribute untold hours of research into Jonestown tapes and journals for the Jonestown Institute at San Diego State University, as well as numerous articles for its annual online publication, *the Jonestown report*. All of Michael's research is available on line: http:/Jonestown.sdsu.edu/

AboutJonestown/Articles/articles_bellefountaine.htm. He also assisted in the transcription of hundreds of audio tapes left by the temple and retrieved by the FBI.

Michael worked for several years researching and writing a book on the gay members of Peoples Temple. Along the way, it encompassed more than that: in telling their stories, he documents what everyone associated with the temple - from those who died in Jonestown, to the survivors and relatives who were deeply affected by the tragedy of November 18, 1978 — and what we can learn from this event.

My son, Michael Bellefountaine, passed away May 10, 2007 at the age of 41. If he had lived this project would have been a more polished piece. This book is a new perspective of the Temple from Michael Bellefountaine ... an activist, a scholar and a proud member of the gay community. This book is his legacy.

Due to Michael's untimely death, I have tried to finish this book on his behalf.

$\mathcal{P}$RINCIPALS

The following people play important roles in *A Lavender Look at the Temple*.

Monica Bagby – Young Los Angeles Peoples Temple member who was wounded trying to leave Jonestown on November 18.

Edith Cordell – Member of Peoples Temple since 1953 and the first Cordell to attend Jones' service, eventually convincing many of her large family to join her new church; died in Jonestown.

Loretta Stewart Cordell Coomer – Wife of one of Edith's many relatives, Harold Cordell. Loretta played the organ for the Temple and helped coordinate the music for the services. After divorcing Harold took the name Coomer. While in Jonestown she was the nighttime nursery supervisor; died in Jonestown.

Cynthia Davis – A Texan who joined the Temple in her early twenties. While in Jonestown, Cynthia worked in the cassava fields and enjoyed taking trips on the community's boat; died in Jonestown.

Jamie Gill – The only known transgender Peoples Temple member.

Vernon Gosney – Vernon was a Peoples Temple member and on November 18, 1978 was wounded trying to escape. His son Mark died in Jonestown.

Pat Grunnett – Temple member who helped coordinate the Jonestown school curriculum; died in Jonestown.

Jim and Marceline Jones – Founders of Peoples Temple; both died in Jonestown.

Teresa King – Temple member from Texas who was fluent in Spanish. She was the librarian in Jonestown and also taught in the community's school system; died in Jonestown.

Garry Lambrev – Garry was the first person to join Peoples Temple after its move to Ukiah, California. He was one of the few people who were able to come and go from the church without being labeled a traitor.

Diane Lundquist – Came from a communist background and joined the Temple along with her sister. Her mother supported her work in the church. Visited her daughter in Jonestown, leaving the morning Leo Ryan arrived; Diane died in Jonestown.

Linda Mertle – Severely beaten as a young Temple member. Linda's father and stepmother founded the Concerned Relatives group, which organized opposition to Jim Jones and the practices of his church.

Harvey Milk – Gay San Francisco City Supervisor, murdered November 27, 1978.

Tobi Stone – Tobi was a tomboy Temple member who worked on the Jonestown construction crew. Tobi hesitated going communal for fear that her children might go without. She overcame her concerns and moved to Jonestown with her two children; died in Jonestown.

Alan Swanson – Joined Peoples Temple after witnessing a healing service. Alan left the church after the discipline evolved to abuse. He was one of the few people who stayed in the Ukiah area, and remained on good terms with the Temple.

John Timmons – Was in the first known sanctioned gay relationship with Garry Lambrev.

Keith Wade – A young Los Angeles member who went to Jonestown with his mother. He introduced Vernon Gosney to Monica Bagby after they each confided in him their desire to leave the community; died in Jonestown.

Deanna Wilkinson – Temple pianist who gave up a singing contract to go to Jonestown. Deanna developed a strong relationship with Loretta Stewart Cordell Coomer that lasted most of the women's lives; died in Jonestown.

$\mathcal{I}$NTRODUCTION

On November 18, 1978 more than nine hundred members of Peoples Temple died at their mission outpost, Jonestown, located in the jungles of Guyana, South America. News reports flashed all over the world about the uneducated, inner-city cult members who mindlessly went into the wilderness and wantonly killed a congressman and then their own children, their elders, and themselves at the command of their messianic and corrupted leader, Jim Jones. So goes the official story of the last hours of Jonestown and, effectively, the last hours of the social movement called Peoples Temple. It's a story that is often recited without variance.

Upon closer inspection, however, one finds Peoples Temple, as a movement, to be far more complex and the members all too human. As one studies the hundreds of photos and reads the various documents from the church, it was clear that the folks who made up the membership of Peoples Temple represented all aspects of American society. Far from being anomalies in American culture, Peoples Temple – as individuals and as the social movement – were a direct product of the intense political movements gripping America during the sixties and seventies. The civil rights movement, the peace movement, the anti-nuclear and pro-environment movements, women's rights, gay rights, race riots, political assassinations and black power all erupted during this turbulent time, and impacted every aspect of American life.

Attracting the compassionate, idealistic, organized and committed, Peoples Temple made folks feel that they were each an individual part of a larger church community actively and directly involved in a movement to reform society by exposing and confronting the race, gender, sex and class based biases inherent in America. They were also building a parallel society void of these social discriminations, a place where everyone would be equal in social status, where they could grow and explore life without the burdensome chains of discrimination and poverty that prohibits many people in America from achieving their full human potential. The promises and dreams were plenty: protection, freedom, escape, personal growth, family, and – what had often been illusive for many – a better future.

The members of Peoples Temple engaged in an active approach to social change. Indiana farmers, college educated youth, California hippies, Viet Nam veterans, and people from all class backgrounds and races came together to help hundreds of inner city families improve their lives in San Francisco and Los Angeles (and to a lesser extent Chicago, Detroit, New York and Philadelphia). With a membership eventually numbering in the thousands, Peoples Temple became a potent political force in the state of California, and was poised to become a nationwide congregation before it moved its base to Jonestown. Indeed no other organization had focused on, organized or mobilized poor people in San Francisco to the degree that Peoples Temple did. It was this passion for racial and economic equality, expressed through vibrant Pentecostal evangelical faith healing services that attracted people from all walks of life to Jim Jones and Peoples Temple.

Unfortunately the membership of Peoples Temple fell into what could only be called a messianic catch-22. Despite the teachings of traditional Jewish and Christian denominations – that the savior is coming in the form of a modern day prophet – any group that actually believes it has found the messiah is ridiculed, scorned, marginalized and discredited. But for Temple members, Jim Jones was simply God personified, and the proof of his godliness was readily apparent in the good works of the communal church.

There were of course problems in Peoples Temple, and many non-members wondered how anyone got involved or stayed with the group after violence and humiliation became part of the church services. Yet every year thousands of college students, presumably better educated than most, join fraternities and sororities whose initiation rites often include beatings and other forms of humiliation. But they join. Temple members who referred to Jim Jones as "Father" and who stayed with him after the allegations of serious misconduct surfaced were often ridiculed. Yet there were literally millions of Catholic Americans who referred to their priests as "Father," and who have stayed with the institution long after others would have left. The folks who joined Peoples Temple were really not so different from other group-oriented Americans.

In addition to being attracted to Jones' politically-charged religious message, Temple members believed that Jim Jones had the power to heal. Faith healing has a long history in American religion; both the American Evangelistic Healers and American Spiritual Healing were nationwide groups with thousands of members. (Ruth Stapleton, the sister of former President Jimmy Carter, toured the country speaking and promoting faith healing, including a stop in San Francisco during the spring of 1977.) Even today, the Centers for Disease Control and the National Institutes of Health are funding studies on the effects of prayer on healing. The elaborate steps taken by Jim Jones to fake various healings are well recorded, but the Temple also went through great lengths to record and document a number of otherwise unexplained healings.

Though many people ridiculed the Temple's faith healing services, they often underestimated those who did believe in them, people who believed they or their loved ones had been healed, as well as those whose lives had truly been healed through one of the Temple's many rehabilitation programs. For many of these people, the Temple helped them at a point in their lives when no one else would, and they responded with an unwavering loyalty and commitment to Jim Jones and Peoples Temple.

As with any large social movement, each Temple member has his or her own story, making one view of Peoples Temple just that: one view. An outsider must try to weave together a tapestry from the stories to begin to get a perception of all the different things Peoples Temple meant to its various members. Because of a range of circumstances, members with similar backgrounds could have vastly different experiences within the Temple. Therefore, though there are some commonalities, it is impossible to peg a white view or black view, or gay view for that matter, in that the experiences of each and every member was unique. This is why each story must be told.

This book focuses on gay and lesbian involvement with Peoples Temple, and how the Temple related to the newly-emerging gay leadership of San Francisco in the late seventies. Did the city's gay and lesbian community interact with Peoples Temple? Did Harvey Milk work with Jim Jones? What was membership in Peoples Temple like for gay men and lesbians? What was life for them like in Jonestown? Did it differ from their heterosexual counterparts; if so, how?

A Lavender Look at the Temple recounts the experiences of a small group of folks within Peoples Temple, chosen primarily because they were involved in the lives of the survivors who agreed to be interviewed. Monica Bagby, Edith Cordell, Loretta Stewart Cordell Coomer, Cynthia Davis, Pat Grunnett, Jamie Gill, Vernon Gosney, Teresa King, Diane Lundquist, Garry Lambrev, Linda Mertle, Tobi Stone, Alan Swanson, John Timmons, Keith Wade and Deanna Wilkinson were all openly gay or lesbian Peoples Temple members. Through their life-stories the reader not only has a first hand account of gay and lesbian Temple experiences, but also discovers what life was like in general for Temple members.

Virtually all aspects of Temple culture are represented in this handful of people. Loretta Stewart Cordell Coomer had been with Jones since his first days of preaching in Indiana, while Pat Grunnett and Garry Lambrev joined during the days in Ukiah. Linda Mertle was brought into the Temple through her parents' involvement and was a youth through her entire Temple experience; Edith Cordell gives voice to the concerns of seniors involved with the group. Cynthia Davis, Tobi Stone, Deanna Wilkinson, and Keith Wade provide the reader with an all too brief glimpses into the lives of African-American gay men and lesbians involved in religious groups. Alan Swanson and John Timmons left Peoples Temple before the mass migration to Jonestown. Vernon Gosney and Monica Bagby were both shot and seriously wounded when they attempted to leave the community with Representative Leo Ryan. Over half of the people on this list died on November 18th.

In addition to the story of gay and lesbian Temple members, this volume documents the connections between gay martyr Harvey Milk and Temple leader Jim Jones. Long obscured and downplayed, a number of letters from Harvey Milk to Jim Jones have been uncovered at the California Historical Society, shedding new light on the close relationship. *A Lavender Look at the Temple* explores the reasons behind Milk's unrelenting support of the church, and details for the first time the relationship between Harvey Milk and Jim Jones.

Initially there was reluctance from some survivors to support this project. Peoples Temple survivors strived to present a unified front, and it seemed disrespectful to start dissecting the group along any lines, whether they were of race, gender or sexual orientation. Understandably some survivors felt that Peoples Temple was marginalized enough and wondered how a gay perspective could portray Temple life accurately or without inviting scorn, perversion and ridicule. However it is important to explore what Peoples Temple was all about, what it stood for, before we can even begin to understand the magnitude of what happened on November 18, 1978. It is irrefutable that the Temple was very pro-gay while it was in the United States, so it makes sense that the gay community would embrace an evaluation of the movement as a whole and lead the way in trying to understand what Peoples Temple was really all about.

Although this book explores the roles these fifteen people played in the Temple, it in no way encompasses all gay or lesbian Temple members' experiences. Sometimes simply asking if someone is gay or lesbian is of such a personal nature, it is taboo to discuss. As a result there are a number of survivors who are not public about their sexuality, unfortunately omitting their important stories from this work. Additionally, unique internal Temple issues convoluted an already confusing issue. For example, there were a number of men who had sex with Jim Jones, but because of the power dynamics within the church, that alone was not enough to indicate homosexuality. Gay men and lesbians got married "for the cause"; straight people "confessed" to homosexual urges. Of course many people simply experimented with sex, not necessarily making them gay or straight. Hopefully for future generations who will explore this subject, Temple members who did not openly identify themselves as gay or lesbian at the time, or who are not out today, will come forward, along with their heterosexual counterparts, and tell their stories to help complete the complex tapestry that is Peoples Temple.

$\mathcal{I}$NDIANAPOLIS, $\mathcal{I}$NDIANA

―――――――――― ✇ ――――――――――

Edith Cordell, Loretta Stewart Cordell

Twenty-year-old Loretta Stewart was devastated by the tragic news. Her mother, Mabel, and five church members had been killed in a car accident on their way home to Indianapolis. They had just attended a service in Cincinnati conducted by their pastor, the Reverend Jim Jones. Among the people killed in the accident was Jones' adopted daughter, Stephanie. Loretta had planned to ride with her mother, but instead opted to go home with a group of friends she had met through the church. The young girl was exceptionally close to her mother, and turned to the church community for comfort through the weeks that followed the tragedy. Jones, whose unique ministry included a claim to paranormal and psychic powers, had warned the group to be careful, that they traveled the road at their own peril. The fulfillment of his prophecy solidified his claim as protector and seer in the eyes of his congregation. Devastated, Loretta devoted herself to her church life. Jones comforted the youth by telling her that her mother would now act as a bridge to the spirit world and enhance his abilities to protect church members, especially from car accidents. Occasionally he was known to tell Loretta that her mother had contacted him with an encouraging message for her.

Mabel Stewart had brought her daughter Loretta to the Laurel Street Tabernacle to see the dynamic preacher and witness the healing services that, along with a message of interracial brotherhood, was the hallmark of Jones' ministry. Loretta enjoyed watching the healings and listening to the testimonials of others who had been cured or saved by Jim Jones. The small church was often packed with over a hundred people, both black and white. The services were a vibrant mix of traditional Midwest evangelical faith

1

healing and inspirational Southern Pentecostal revival. Loretta loved the old fashioned gospel music and took advantage of an opportunity to play the organ and sing for Jones' services.

Loretta caught the eye of Harold Cordell, who was a few years her senior. Harold came to the church because his relative, Edith Cordell, had encouraged all of her large farm family to attend the Tabernacle's services and see Jim Jones. The Cordells had been raised in the traditional Pentecostal church so popular in rural Indiana. Edith was enamored with Jones ever since she saw him on her doorstep selling pet monkeys. She had a good dose of common sense and needed a monkey like she needed a tornado, but before she knew what she was doing, she found herself happily paying Jones for not one monkey but two. Jones told Edith that he was selling the monkeys to raise money for his ministry and invited Edith to come to one of the services at the Laurel Street Tabernacle. Edith, who had been single her whole life, was not partial to men, but she was impressed with this man who talked about how the apostle Paul was a tent maker who worked during the day and preached at night. She agreed that working in the real world would give many ministers a taste of what life was like for everyone else. But here was Jones, wearing used clothes and working to raise money for his own church. She was so impressed she attended the next Laurel Street service.

Edith loved the vibrant music of the healing service. The congregation was close knit, but still open and welcoming. She continued to attend, and was called up to the front of the church and asked to take a sip of water from the fountain by the altar. When Edith sipped the water, it had miraculously turned to wine. She no longer felt the painful arthritis that had been plaguing her for years. Edith became an immediate and loyal convert. She was proud to stand up during future testimonials and tell the congregation of the miracles she had witnessed. A large number of Edith's extended family soon began to accompany her to the little Tabernacle.

The Laurel Street Tabernacle was a church on decline, with an aging minister and no one trained to take over the post. The church's council was impressed with the size of the crowd that Jones could draw, but they were equally turned off by its color. After much debate the church elders decided that Jones' outspoken stance toward blacks would only result in negative publicity for the church, so they did not offer him the permanent position. Jones left the Tabernacle, taking over a half of the congregation with him. Jones and his wife Marceline started a new church called the Wings of Deliverance, and he continued to preach his fiery brand of social commentary.

In 1955, Jones changed the name of his church from the Wings of Deliverance to Peoples Temple Full Gospel Church. The name change signified Jones' desire to have his congregation open to all people. The welcoming interracial church served as a refuge for many people who had been disenfranchised, marginalized, or simply excluded from existing churches. Jones' congregation was unique in that it was a truly interracial group; while many white churches did valuable work in the civil rights movement, they often perpetuated racism by being, acting and by being identified as "white churches" fighting for civil rights for blacks. At Peoples Temple, on the other hand, the membership reflected people of all ages, both black and white, worshipping together.

When the Jones family adopted a black son, they became the first white couple in Indiana to do so. Marceline Jones was often confronted with overt hostility from people in stores and schools, who thought the baby was biologically hers. Jones was said to have integrated local hospitals and churches with a firebrand of direct action. According to one report, he packed up his congregation and went across town to hold a sit-in at another church that was refusing entry to blacks. Other accounts speak of his refusal to go to the white side of a hospital emergency room and demanded to be treated by a black doctor. Peoples Temple is reported to have had the first interracial congregation in Indiana and the first interracial choir in the Midwest.

Jim Jones called Peoples Temples' religious philosophy Apostolic Socialism, the belief that everything should be shared in an environment of true equality between races, genders, ages, and classes. The Temple took its inspiration – and biblical foundation – from Matthew 25: "I was hungry and you fed me, thirsty and you gave me drink; I was a stranger and you received me in your homes, naked and you clothed me; I was sick and you took care of me, in prison and you visited me." The verses appeared on the church's stationery and were often quoted by Jones from the pulpit. More than that, they echoed throughout Temple history, forming the basis of the progressive organization's philosophy, which embraced Christian communal living, socialism, and Jones' definition and interpretation of communism.

Jones' political career was launched with his appointment to the Human Rights Commission in Indianapolis in February 1961. But his high profile also brought unwanted attention. Outraged at the active interracial church, locals began harassing Temple members on the streets and vandalizing Temple buildings. Animals belonging to Temple members started turning up dead. Jones was able to use this harassment to his advantage by building bonds between his members with a feeling of enlightenment and solidarity while fending off overt hostility. He played the role of father protector well. Later, he would be accused of planning much of the vandalism against the Temple to garner community support and sympathy for his congregation.

Deanna Wilkinson

Loretta Stewart married Harold Cordell, and the couple had five bright, blond-haired, blue-eyed children in rapid succession. Loretta devoted herself to singing and playing for Peoples Temple services. Over time she trained a number of other church members in the traditional gospel music. One of those members was a young black girl named Deanna Wilkinson. Deanna had a rare singing talent which captivated anyone who heard it; as an adult she would eventually turn down a professional singing contract. A street-smart kid with multiple burn scars on her face, Deanna had been found severely injured as a newborn in a state park in the Chicago area. She was removed from her parents' custody and put into a foster home with Alice Moton and her family, who regularly attended Jones' services. She had found a family with the Motons and the Motons found a home with the Jones family. Deanna overcame her discomfort of being stared at and began to exhibit her rare natural singing abilities. As she grew, she also played piano alongside Loretta Stewart Cordell and helped her coordinate the Temple's music.

In January 1962, Jim Jones left Indiana to do missionary work in Brazil. While there, he had a vision that a number of US cities, including Indianapolis, were going to be destroyed by nuclear war, and when he returned to Indiana after two years in Brazil, he began preaching of imminent nuclear annihilation.

In the meantime, *Esquire* magazine published an article in its January 1962 issue which claimed that Ukiah, California – about 90 miles north of San Francisco – would be one of the few places in the world safe from potential nuclear fallout. In 1965 Jones packed up his family, including a number of adopted children of various races, and moved to the secluded California community. Eighty members of his interracial Indianapolis-based church followed him there, including Edith Cordell, Harold Cordell, his wife Loretta and their young family. Alice Moton, on the other hand, was too established to just pick up roots and move. She liked to hear the black assistant pastor, Archie Ijames, preach, but she was not inclined to leave her job and move all the way to California, so Deanna Wilkinson stayed behind in Indianapolis.

$\mathcal{U}$KIAH, $\mathcal{C}$ALIFORNIA

Garry Lambrev

$\mathcal{T}he$ first person to stumble on to Peoples Temple in Ukiah was a young man named Garry Lambrev, who moved to the rural community from Palo Alto to take a job at the Welfare Department. He was 22 years old and had been politically active while a student. One of the promises he made to himself was to be open to any opportunities for political action in his new community.

One morning he walked from his office to the local courthouse and spotted an old clunker car with a Phil Drath sticker on it. Drath, a Quaker running for Congress on an antiwar platform, had few visible supporters in the area. Garry approached the car, which was sitting at a red light in the center of town. He asked the driver, a heavyset, blue-collar-type woman, if there were any antiwar activities in the area. To his surprise neither the woman, who stared straight ahead, nor her passenger, a well-dressed older gentleman, said anything. The light turned green and the car sped away, leaving Garry puzzled in the middle of the small-town intersection.

As he turned to go to his office, he heard a yell from the old car and saw a hand stretch out from the driver's side window, first tossing a number of fliers and then bumper stickers on to the street. Embarrassed, he quickly picked up the political literature and hurried back to his office at the Welfare Department. He was at his desk for only a few minutes before he got word that someone was there to see him. He went to the side door to see the driver of the old car. Patty Cartmell laughed as she explained she had been taking a driving test when Garry approached the car. She needed a license to take a job to help support her family, who had recently moved to California with her pastor. She had been hesitant to express her antiwar views in front of the driving inspector, and noticed that Garry had gone into the welfare office as she pulled into the adjacent parking lot. "Funny thing though," she remarked. "My pastor told me something unusual would happen during my driving test, but not to worry, I would pass the test. He really is amazing." And so Garry Lambrev first heard of the prophetic, psychic powers of Reverend Jim Jones.

Patty Cartmell was as faithful to Jim Jones and Peoples Temple as a person could be, and she was happy to ask Garry to join her family for Friday dinner. New to the area, and with few social contacts, he accepted Patty's offer. He was immediately impressed with the accepting, non-traditional family that lived its politics; it was the community he had been long looking for. As he was introduced to key members of the multi-racial extended family of Peoples Temple, he recognized a social model that might work for the whole country, a transformation that could finally eliminate poverty and promote racial harmony. All he had to do was join the Temple.

Garry was invited to a Temple Youth Dance later that evening at the cabin of a young couple, Harold and Loretta Stewart Cordell. Garry was glad to accompany his new friends, Joyce Beam and Patty Cartmell's son Mike. The cabin was heated by a wood stove in the center of the room, and kerosene lamps gave off a faint glow. Approximately twenty teens and as many adult chaperones danced and swayed to soul music. Garry soon found himself engaged in the most profound conversation of his life with a chaperone standing against the wall, a man whose name he didn't immediately catch. After twenty minutes or so, Garry asked him his name. The man introduced himself as Jim Jones, the pastor of Peoples Temple.

Jones had a unique ability to connect with each and every member of his congregation, making them feel as though they shared a special relationship. Garry certainly felt it. After the long conversation, Jones told the young man he was welcome to join the church, but that he would be wasting his talents at Peoples Temple. Garry wasn't sure if Jones sensed his rebellious spirit, or was using a bit of reverse psychology, but Garry was so impressed with the integrated community, he quickly accepted an invitation to attend the Temple's weekend service.

That Sunday Garry attended the Peoples Temple service with a childhood friend, Gerry. The congregation had just under a hundred members. The service centered around Jones' sermons on a social gospel for contemporary America, interspersed with singing and testimonials. Garry was surprised when, fifteen minutes into the sermon, Jim Jones began to preach about homosexuals and their influence in the antiwar movement. Jones talked about James Baldwin, and the gay and lesbian leaders of the War Resisters League. Garry was amazed at how welcoming and supportive the church was to homosexuals. Even in the progressive movements of the time, the role of queers was pretty much overlooked. Certainly coming out in this church would be completely different than coming out in a traditional Christian denomination. Garry's friend had an opposite reaction to the Temple's service. Gerry respected the works of Peoples Temple, and even admired their goals, but the country-bumpkin fundamentalists from the Bible belt were too much for him to take. Garry on the other hand felt he had stumbled into something monumental and historic. Nobody had to tell him what was going on. He could see it and feel it, and desperately wanted to become part of it.

The following week Garry brought another friend to the Temple. Audrey was so impressed with Peoples Temple, she soon found herself regularly commuting to church functions from her job and home in Los Altos, more than 150 miles away. At Audrey's first meeting (and Garry's second), Jim Jones gave them both an important assignment: they were to organize Ukiah's first antiwar protest. The work was important and no one else was doing it. Jones told them they could use the Temple resources to plan a march and a rally. So they did.

The next day, Audrey told Garry about a dream she had in which she was being followed by a man with a crew cut. Days before the protest she actually saw the man she described from her dream – "about as drably anonymous as Lee Harvey Oswald," as Garry recalls – complete with crew cut. The protest had gotten a small amount of press, and Garry and Audrey had applied for the necessary permits. In a town the size of Ukiah, word travels fast, so the man could have been from anywhere, any agency, or a random kook.

Jim Jones went to Mexico with Temple member Joe Phillips to scout for potential mission sites, and was not planning to be back in time for the rally. Garry and Audrey approached Marceline Jones with their concerns about the person who had them under surveillance. She informed them that she had just spoken to Jones and he told her, "I know that Garry and Audrey are worried about the event, but they shouldn't be. Everything will be all right." To the uninitiated, this would be just a simple, if not predictable, statement of support, but to Garry and Audrey, who believed Jones had the power of prophecy, this was the green light they needed to proceed.

After only a week of organizing, they had everything in order for the rally. On Good Friday about a hundred people, most of them Peoples Temple members, marched a mile and a half down State Street in Ukiah, carrying a coffin draped in black and a US flag. The march ended at the steps to the county courthouse, and as Garry began speaking to the crowd; Audrey spotted the man from her dream headed toward the crowd and up the steps. Garry immediately felt a protective wall surround him. As the man aggressively approached Garry, he came to a dead stop right where Garry envisioned his protective wall. "Though he seemed to struggle and his face turned red, he simply couldn't move beyond that point" Garry recalls. At that moment Jim Jones waded into the group from the opposite direction, electrifying the crowd of Temple members. The Temple leader also climbed the steps, his eye fixed on the intruder, and, as Garry says, "the man who had seemed so threatening moments ago quickly retreated and was soon lost to sight. The 'truth,' verified to me years later by Joe Phillips, was that Jim suddenly had a vision of us being attacked while they were driving through the desert of Sonora, still heading south, and decided instantly to turn back."

Garry was convinced he was in the presence of someone truly gifted with prophecy. He was hooked. By August 1966, Garry Lambrev, a gay welfare worker, became the first person to officially join Peoples Temple since it relocated to California in the fall of 1965.

Jones later contacted Walter Heady, leader of the local John Birch society, complaining about the surveillance of his group. The meeting led to a political relationship of cordiality and respect between the men.

In late 1968, after three intense years with the church, Garry told Jones he wanted to leave because he felt his creativity was being stymied. More to the point, he wanted to explore the burgeoning gay counterculture of San Francisco. Jones was not pleased to lose such a creative and industrious member, and cautioned Garry that his karma would become crude and corrupted, and that all the good work he had done for the Temple would be washed away. Jones warned Garry that the world was changing, that he should rightfully fear what was out there. He went on to tell Garry of a rampant epidemic that by implication might inhibit any plans for a promiscuous lifestyle. If Garry were to leave the aura of the church, he faced a life of drugs and disease. Years later, not long after the Jonestown tragedy, when he first heard of the "AIDS epidemic," he recalled the prophetic words of Jim Jones. But at the time he would not be deterred. He left the Temple and worked as a field hand in Ukiah.

More than two years later, disenchanted with a drug-drenched culture that had mired him in addiction and loneliness, Garry longed to return to the supportive environment of Peoples Temple. He soon found himself back at Temple functions, only to eventually want to leave again. But Garry never left on bad terms with the Temple, and was one of only a few people who frequently left and returned to the church.

Garry was assigned to edit *The Living Word,* the Temple's promotional magazine informational pamphlet. The Temple used each edition for outreach and fundraising, telling of various prophecies and healings by Jim Jones. In keeping with Ukiah's more conservative audience, *The Living Word* was less political and more religiously oriented than future publications would be, but nevertheless folded after several issues. When the Temple moved to San Francisco, it launched another newspaper called *The Peoples Forum*, but by that time, Garry had left once again, this time to pursue a relationship with his childhood friend Gerry.

Jim Jones had an amazing ability to use the Bible to support his evolving political and religious beliefs. He combined his biblical knowledge with claims of paranormal and psychic ability, and was adept at pulling passages that talked about healings, communal living, helping the downtrodden and recognizing the equality between all people. Heaven was a lie, Jones said, told to poor people to keep them complacent in this abusive world. People needed to band together and build heaven here on earth.

Jones also used the Bible to point out the flaws in what he called "your black book." Garry worked on the production of "The Letter Killeth" which outlined the contradictions in the King James Version of the Bible. Jones used this publication to show people how they had been deceived. Most of those who attended Peoples Temple had grown up with Christian piety and orthodoxy, and often had never heard anyone talk so openly about the many contradictions in the Bible. Jones' candor about the contradictions only served as further proof to his followers that he was revealing a truth which their former pastors had either ignored or glossed over.

John Timmons

Garry Lambrev met John Timmons at a gay bar in the Castro district of San Francisco. Garry brought John to the Temple, eventually becoming the first sanctioned gay couple in the church. However, Temple stalwart Penny Dupont found the gay men troublesome and did everything she could to break them up. But when the topic was brought up to Jim Jones, Penny lost out, and the gay relationship won the approval of the Temple leadership. The relationship failed, as sometimes they do, but it was the first, openly accepted gay male coupling in Peoples Temple. John Timmons left Peoples Temple soon after the break-up.

Linda Mertle

Al and Deanna Mertle were married in 1968 and settled into the Bay Area with their new family, including five children, two children from her previous marriage, three from his. Together they faced the same challenges as many young couples, including marijuana use by Al's 10-year-old daughter, Linda. Al and Deanna were invited to their first temple service by their minister. He had heard about the healing services and drug rehab programs of the dynamic church in Ukiah, invited Al and Deanna to their first Temple service. They were immediately welcomed, and drawn to the passionate members and socially progressive programs sponsored by the church. After a few return trips, the Mertle family joined Peoples Temple on November 2, 1969, commuting from their small farm in Hayward, over three hours away.

Growing up in the Temple, Linda played games focused on cooperation instead of competition, roamed the woods, fields, orchards and vineyards, rode the ponies owned by the Temple and took snorkeling lessons in the swimming pool. She had immediate friends and family, a real sense of belonging. But she also had an incredible amount of fear: she was afraid of Jim Jones. Indeed, what ten-year-old would not be frightened in the presence of the living God? She firmly believed Jones had the power to read minds, which usually was enough to keep her in line though she sometimes broke the rules anyway. She witnessed a number of healings, but also a number of disciplines that truly scared her. Although the pool brought up images of baptisms, pool parties and snorkeling lessons, it also was the place of incredible cruelty. Linda watched a number of people hog-tied and thrown into the pool as punishment for various infractions.

Al and Deanna Mertle moved to Redwood Valley to be closer to the church. Both of them were promoted to the Planning Commission, the church's organizing body, assuming more and more responsibilities within the organization. Deanna began working on publicity, and both she and Al ran the church's concession stand selling photos of Jones and various trinkets such as lockets and prayer cloths. The Temple used the Mertles' large home to house a number of people, including Linda's good friend, Nichol Johnson. By the time she turned fourteen, it became clear to Linda that she was a lesbian, but unlike most queer kids being raised in religious communities, she faced no bigotry from her church counterparts. It was against the rules for the children to ridicule or tease others. On the other hand, like many queer youth, she faced a father who was not happy that his little girl was growing up to be a dyke.

While in Ukiah, the Temple's schedule became all-consuming for its members. Jones kept them on the move, with exhausting meetings that went as late as three or four in the morning. By 1970, the Temple also began holding recruitment and outreach services in neighboring cities and towns. Soon Temple meetings were being held in Los Angeles and San Francisco, with occasional trips as far as Seattle, Washington and Portland, Oregon. Linda's stepmother Deanna – who changed her name to Jeannie Mills after she left the Temple – described Temple life to one author:

Mrs. Mills remembers well the typical weekly schedule at Peoples

Temple in Redwood Valley. 'Sunday there was always a meeting from eleven am to three pm,' she explained. 'We would meet again from six pm on Sunday until approximately three or four in the morning on Monday. Then we would all go to work, sleeping when and if we could. The Planning Commission (which included over one hundred people) met on Monday nights from seven pm until about seven am the next morning.

Wednesday night there was a meeting that lasted from seven pm until at least two or three am on Thursday morning. Friday night there was a meeting in San Francisco that lasted from seven pm until about one am. Then we got into one of the eleven Greyhound busses and drove to Los Angeles (which took at least seven hours); and we would try to sleep as we rode.

We would arrive in Los Angeles in time for the two pm afternoon meeting, which lasted until about six pm. We would have dinner. The next meeting would start at seven thirty pm and last until at least one or two am. We would assemble after that public meeting for a planning session that lasted the rest of the night until about eight am in the morning. Our Sunday service would go from eleven am until four pm and we would then ride back to Redwood Valley in time to go to school or work the next day.

Despite the self-contradiction of giving two different itineraries for Sunday, and the fact that the schedule for the general membership would not include meetings for the Planning Commission, one still gets an idea of how much time Temple members spent at church. Whether Temple members spent Sunday in Ukiah meetings or traveling home from Los Angeles, they still spent a considerable amount of time working on Temple projects and going to various meetings.

As author Mel White points out:

Just to illustrate how much time Jones spent influencing the beliefs of his followers, compare how much time you have spent in church in the past ten years. If you have averaged two hours a week in worship or study you have been exposed to roughly a thousand hours of content time. Subtract time loss passing around attendance sheets, listening to announcements, taking offerings, getting 'settled down,' catching up with last weeks lesson, drinking punch or eating cookies (as well as time lost to vacations, illness, or just playing hooky) you will be fortunate to have spent five hundred hours in ten years in increasing your

Christian education at church. Jones had that much time to influence members of the Temple every ten weeks.

In addition to dominating the Temple members' time and money, Jones began to manipulate them sexually as well. In 1971, after a cross-country trip to the Father Divine Peace Mission in Philadelphia, Jones expanded his earlier theory that sex was a needless self-indulgence that served as a distraction from the movement. The only love people needed could be derived from the cause and all the good work that they were doing. There was no time for self-indulgent sex when you are literally battling for salvation and freedom. Many people had also been manipulated or hurt through sex at some point in their lives, causing them to confuse sex with love. Jones preached that a person would know the difference between love and lust if no sex were involved. One needed to shed the desire for sex to discover the true meaning of love. The Bible said that God is love, Jones preached, and therefore love must be God. People should strive to substitute the love they once had for a lover and transfer it to all humankind. However, he did realize the power of human attraction, and the Temple accepted sexual relationships among its members as a necessity to keep the weak loyal. But the goal for everyone – gay and straight – was to live a life free of sexual desire.

The sublimation of sexuality undoubtedly contributed to a new message that members heard from the Temple pulpit. As Judith Weightman writes:

By '74 [Jones] began to preach that he alone, among Temple members and women, was the only true heterosexual. All the rest were hiding their homosexuality, he declared: having heterosexual relations was simply a masquerade. Perhaps out of shame for homosexual tendencies within himself, Jones made his members publicly admit homosexual feelings or acts, past and present, latent or overt ... And he personally had sex with some men in his church, ostensibly to prove to them their own homosexuality.

A number of Temple members interviewed for this book agreed with Weightman's assessment, but they believe her timeline was off. They recalled Jones taught as early as 1966, that everyone had homosexual feelings.

It is not clear what Jones meant when he said that he was the only true heterosexual or where exactly he fit into a world full of lesbians. Nevertheless, many people confessed or acknowledged homosexual feelings at a time when you could still lose your job for being identified as a gay man or lesbian. Was it just a ploy to humiliate and emasculate macho heterosexual men? Or did Jones truly feel that everyone struggles with the issue of homosexuality, though few people are ready to acknowledge such self-inspection?

As Jeannie Mills recalls:

The Planning Commission meetings were often used as Jim's testing grounds. If a new idea worked on us, he would try it in the public meetings. Even his homosexual activities were going to be shared with the rest of the church members. In explanation to an attorney, who strongly suggested that he should keep this part of his life quiet, Jim explained, 'If people were to find out about this through some other source, they would never forgive me. However, if I tell them myself, and explain that I am doing it for the Cause, no matter what they hear from anyone else, they won't feel that I have betrayed them.'

Sure enough, at the next Sunday service Jim broached the subject of his homosexual acts. 'One young man here was having problems relating to the Cause, and he asked me to relate to him in a more personal way. Even though I find homosexuality disgusting, if one of my members needs me to minister to them on any level, I will not refuse them. However, this man was most inconsiderate when he came to me without first having cleansed himself.' He was looking directly at Randy, one of the guards, who was standing near the front in full view of the audience, 'that person who begged me to do something that I find completely foreign to my own natural desires should have at least taken an enema before he came to me.'

It was apparent to almost everyone there that he had been talking about Randy, both by the blush Randy had just acquired and by the fact that Jim was staring at him. In deep humiliation Randy stood up, raised his head, and said, 'That's true, Father, and I apologize for being so thoughtless.'

Jim had accomplished what he wanted. He had been the first to tell his members that he was having sex with men and he had made it sound as if it had been nasty and disgusting to him.

Jim's sermons began to be filled with discussions about sex. He was changing his own sexual practices and seemed to need to justify it in his meetings. 'Every man is a homosexual and every woman is a lesbian. I am the only man alive that really knows how to make a woman happy. Every man wants to have a dick up his ass and every woman wants to suck another woman's pussy.' The first time Jim talked like this, people were shocked, but like everything else he did, after a few times, it ceased to be shocking.

Mills tells of other incidents in which Jones confronted men about their need to have sex with him. He told the congregation that he had thrown up on the back of the first man he had sex with, but – as Jones described it – the man needed it, so Jones obliged. (How this helped the young man remains unclear.) Both men and women were humiliated and embarrassed publicly after having sexual relationships with Jones. Mills conveyed an example of the complex games Jones played:

After he degraded a few more people, Jim looked around room to see who he had missed. He asked, 'How many people in here have had sex with me?'

About twenty people, both men and women, stood. Jim looked at a man named Harry, who was sitting quietly, looking out the window, and said, 'Someone in here is ashamed to admit that he asked me to have sex with him. But you sure weren't ashamed when you were squealing with delight as we were fucking the other night were you, Harry?'

Harry jumped up quickly and apologized. 'I thought you didn't want me to mention that, so I didn't stand. I'm not shamed of what we did.'

Jim smiled at Harry. 'Well I just don't want anyone thinking they're special to me. You are all special whether I fuck you or not.'

Mills' account of Jones' sexual pronouncements and interactions is supported by other Temple members. Laurie Efrein Kahalas recounts how confused she was by the evolving importance of sexually relating to Jones. For Kahalas, the interactions were not rooted in traditional gay-straight love based relationships, but were far more complex:

The protection Jim Jones opted for psychologically, was the conviction that he was always the giver and others the takers – obviously disempowering to the taker, who can never freely love, but must remain a dependant child! I would finally surmise that 'everyone needs a father' and 'People need a father more than they need sex,' had more to do with his relating across sexual lines, than any inherent homosexuality in either him or most of the men. The model wasn't man/woman. It was parent/child ... Jim said people don't really want sex anyway. They want a father. "So what was this, mass incest?" I could never, ever ask. No one could.

Despite Jones' claims of only having homosexual sex with his followers because they demanded it, his support for gay people and opposition to police stings may have been more personal in nature. By the seventies, large city police forces had perfected the art of shaking down and harassing the gay community. Before the advent of the 1980's gay bar culture scene, parks, theaters, and other public places were areas where gay men could meet each other. Vice squads continually raided well-known gay meeting places as well as the first gay bars. The raids usually involved rounding up twenty to fifty men, beating the drunkest, loudest and most scared, and issuing citations for future court dates or fines to be paid on the spot. In the worst cases, the offenders' names were listed in the local press, jeopardizing jobs and humiliating family members. Large vice offices employed numerous decoys to trap gay men in parks, theaters, and public restrooms, a form of harassment that continues in a number of cities today.

On December 13, 1973, two undercover male cops arrested Jim Jones at the Westlake Theater in Los Angeles for exposing himself, and charged him with lewd conduct. Though the case quietly went away after a few months and the arrest subsequently sealed by a judge, the incident is a clear indicator of Jones' sexual tastes outside of Peoples Temple, and presumably devoid of the power factor that came into play when Jones was sexual with other Temple members. This is not to say Jones was gay. Indeed, most men who go to theaters or parks are closeted gay men or bisexuals who would not be seen going into an exclusively gay identified establishment, such as a gay bar. However, after being directly involved in a gay sting set up, Jones' solidarity with gay men may have been more than rhetorical.

Alan Swanson

In1970, 25-year-old Alan Swanson was one of the thousands of gay men drawn to the freedom of the emerging San Francisco gay scene. A number of Alan's friends had joined one of the many Jesus groups that were springing up around the late sixties and early seventies. The small group of friends eventually moved to Seattle to escape life in modern Sodom. Renouncing their homosexuality, the group joined an evangelical-based commune in the Seattle area. In an attempt to save the gay community, members of the commune would go to various bathhouses and gay bars and put up "Jesus Saves" or "Jesus Loves You" stickers.

A next-door neighbor, an elderly woman who was known to be very generous in the neighborhood collecting clothes and food for the needy, asked the commune members if they would join her to go see a visiting Native American preacher, who was also a healer. (Jim Jones claimed Native American ancestry to build solidarity with his non-white congregants.) Alan joined the group and was amazed by the Temple service. A number of people were called to the front of the church and healed of various ailments, from arthritis to cancer. As the group returned home, they discussed the healings, expressing disappointment that the congregation attributed the successful healings to Jones, instead of giving the credit to God. Though the group liked the show, they decided to cancel plans to attend a second service the following evening. Alan decided to return alone.

At the second meeting, Alan was genuinely surprised when Jones announced from the podium, "There is someone here who has a friend named Ron Sims. Ron Sims is in trouble and I need that friend to come forward and receive this prayer cloth. You must give it to Ron to protect him from future danger. Could the friend of Ron Sims come forward?" Alan knew a Ron Sims, and knew his friend was on hard times, so he stepped forward and received the prayer cloth. Alan now fully believed Jones had prophetic powers. The atmosphere of the meeting was electrifying, as other members of the congregation were called forward and given personal revelations.

Jones then moved on to the healing portion of the service. A black woman sitting next to Alan had been diagnosed with cancer and had written to Jones asking if he would be willing to see her. Jones called her forward, and asked her if she had enough faith to pass the cancer. Cheers and applause from the congregation punctuated every response to Jones' questions. Nurses closed in around the woman, briefly blocking Alan's view, and then one of the nurses emerged, holding up a bloody mass. The room erupted with ecstasy with the witness of another miracle. That was all Alan needed to be convinced. This preacher wore used clothes, did not own a car, obviously had prophetic ability, and seemingly had the power to heal.

Alan returned to the commune to tell his friends what he had experienced and asked them to give Jones another chance. His friends refused. He wanted to go and check out the Temple's headquarters in California, and asked a woman he knew to join him. She also refused. So Alan packed his bags, said goodbye to his friends and made his way to Ukiah. There he rented a small cottage and found outside work in addition to his Temple job, to bring in extra income. He began to get adjusted into his new life in California.

Even though the Temple was based in Ukiah, members limited their participation in the larger community to holding jobs to bring in much needed money. Everyone was discouraged from interacting with the general public. The self-imposed isolation of individual members relaxed in the early 1970s, when Jones began encouraging them to live communally. The Temple leader quoted from the Bible to support his teachings of communal living, reminding people that the Bible teaches people to hold all things in common and that the church's role is to take care of the faithful.

The Temple's multiple outreach services and politically-charged sermons attracted bright, college-educated, middle-class young adults to the dynamic multi-racial congregation. In addition to its weekly public meetings the Temple held numerous meetings closed to non-members. This distance from the general public gave the church a certain mystique, a sense of exception and exclusivity. Various degrees of membership evolved: there were those who donated all of their possessions to work and live exclusively in the Temple, those who held down outside jobs and donated a portion of their income to the church but who retained whatever property they might have, and still other, more peripheral members, attended functions and public services.

Pat Grunnett

Pat Grunnett was the quintessential 70s California girl: socially conscious, politically active, her pastimes included macramé, ceramics, woodcarving and the guitar. Pat typified the person who came to the Temple while it was based in Ukiah. She was passionate about her politics, well educated and painfully aware of her privileged status in American society. Interviewed in September 1978, Pat recalled, "While still in college, I spent vacations taking groups of middle-class white kids to Indian reservations and San Joaquin Valley depressed minority areas to work with the people in order to expose them to the culture of poverty. We painted, planted, built, played, and worked with the folks there, said we'd never forget them, and then went right back behind the white picket fences and birch trees in our own communities."

As a child Pat was very sickly. The doctors were so unsure of her survival that they delayed filling out her birth certificate. After numerous life-threatening operations, she surprised everyone by not only surviving but by eventually excelling academically. Her bouts of bad health were compounded from a sexual assault by a respected pastor that led to feelings of isolation and distrust. Her father also blamed her for his failings, making her feel as though her medical costs had ruined the family financially. She worked her way through college, oftentimes sending money home to help support her family.

Unsatisfied and unfulfilled, Pat Grunnett left America after graduating from college to work for the Peace Corps in Africa where she became fluent in Swahili. After three years of teaching in Africa, she returned home and submerged herself in her work for social change, including the war resistance movement, prison and education reform, and in support of Cesar Chavez and the rights of migrant farm workers.

In 1972, a co-worker of Pat recommended she seek legal help from Peoples Temple for a Latino client who was facing felony charges. As Pat recalled, "The whole church rallied around us, and the moral support we received from letters and assurances meant a great deal to us. Jim spoke of all the things I'd wanted to be part of in an effectual way. Here was the community. They were accomplishing what I wanted to be a part of; led by the most incredible strategist I'd ever heard of. My days of playing at changing things were over. Now we're doing it." Pat Grunnett was no longer alone. She'd found what she was looking for: a welcoming family actively working for effective social change. She was an immediate and loyal convert.

Loretta Stewart Cordell Coomer, Deanna Wilkinson

During the summer, Temple buses would take hundreds of members across the country, often passing through Washington, DC for a day of lobbying. When the summer ended, the Temple again focused its outreach in the western region of the country. During the tour in 1970, the Temple's bus convoy passed through its hometown of Indianapolis, where Deanna Wilkinson decided to leave the Moton family and join the cross country tour back to California.

As Peoples Temple settled in Ukiah, Harold and Loretta Stewart Cordell became more and more distant. They each found their own roles in the Temple and spent less time together. Eventually they decided to an amicable divorce. Loretta, well-liked and popular with the general congregation, occupied her time by caring for her children, playing the organ and working with pianist Deanna Wilkinson on the music for Temple services. Harold, also well-liked, began a relationship with Edith Bogue. Loretta and Deanna were old friends, and Loretta was surprised how much the little girl she remembered had grown up into a strong, passionate, proud black woman with the most amazing voice around.

In one of her many letters to her family, Temple member Annie Moore wrote about working with Loretta and Deanna: "I've been practicing the piano a lot. Did you know that I am getting taught lessons from our church organist and the pianist? They want me to be able to play if they need a fill-in sometime. It's really neat because it's that gospel-type stuff and the pianist (who does most of my teaching) sings just like Aretha Franklin and plays better than any of those people on the radio. I feel really fortunate to be able to learn from her. She refused an offer to go big time, just so she could play for the church."

Loretta Stewart Cordell changed her name to Loretta Coomer, and began working for Patty Cartmell and her husband, Walter, who managed the Ukiah Answering Services, was considered by many to be the nerve center of the small town. A number of Temple members staffed the office, allowing Jones to keep his finger on the pulse of the community.

Vernon Gosney

In Seattle, Washington, 1972, Vernon and Cheryl Gosney, a young bi-racial couple, found a flier on their car announcing a Peoples Temple's faith healing service. Faith healing intrigued Gosney and his wife, and they eagerly looked forward to attending. Initially, the Gosneys were overwhelmed by the welcome they received, so completely different from what they were accustomed to. After the dynamic service, the Gosneys decided to check out the Temple's main church in Ukiah. Within a few months of commuting from Seattle, Cheryl and Vernon Gosney moved to California to be closer to Peoples Temple.

Tobi Stone

Tobi Stone was a young black woman who was brought into the Temple by her friends, Marie Duckett and Chris Lewis. A tomboy who would often be confused as a boy, Tobi was the mother of two children. Although others saw her as a dynamic, out, tough, butch dyke, she referred to herself as a quiet, shy girl, almost to the point of being timid. At one point she referred to herself as "extremely nervous by nature." This anxiety was compounded by persistent eye trouble which a childhood operation had not resolved. She first learned of Peoples Temple in 1970, eventually becoming a member in 1974. Tobi too felt a sense of security and loyalty in the small church family and found a place where she could feel she was part of something big, while still maintaining her privacy and inner space.

Peoples Temple expanded into California's major metropolitan areas of San Francisco and Los Angeles, at first holding services in schools or rented auditoriums, later purchasing large churches. In 1973, Peoples Temple moved its headquarters from Ukiah to their new church located on Geary Boulevard, between Fillmore and Steiner Streets, in one of the most impoverished, depressed neighborhoods in San Francisco.

San Francisco, California

--- ⊞ ---

Loretta Stewart Cordell Coomer, Deanna Wilkinson

Loretta Stewart Cordell Coomer and Deanna Wilkinson had never been busier with the Temple music. Honing and updating various songs, the pianist and organist developed into quite a team. The two began to spend a great deal of time together and forged a loving friendship based on loyalty and trust that would last their lifetimes. Unfortunately Loretta began feeling sick, and was diagnosed with breast cancer resulting in surgery. Like many members of Peoples Temple, her health problems brought her closer to Jim Jones and the church community. Many felt they would have been sicker or even dead if it were not for the Temple and Jones' protective aura.

As part of its outreach to the impoverished Fillmore district, Peoples Temple ran a free medical clinic in a brick building owned by Dr. Carlton Goodlett, Jr., the Temple's most dedicated supporter in the African American community. The clinic offered free pap smears, sickle cell anemia tests, pre-natal and neo-natal care and other preventive care usually unobtainable for the neighborhood's residents. Temple members were sent to medical and dental school, and eventually the church included a rather large number of nurses among its members. While many congregants believed they no longer needed to go to a doctor – because the aura of Jim Jones would keep them free from getting sick – the church's leadership encouraged them to seek medical care, if for no other reason than to confirm one of Jones' healings.

In addition to the modern clinic, Peoples Temple used its considerable resources to bring about unprecedented community-based change in the Fillmore neighborhood. The Temple sponsored day and evening care for both children and seniors of the community. It maintained a "cold turkey" drug and alcohol rehabilitation program, which succeeded in transferring troubled teens out of the legal system and into church programs. Temple members would show up in large numbers – oftentimes filling the courtrooms with supporters – for court dates and hearings to support the youths. Lawyers from the church would petition judges to assume responsibility for the youths, guaranteeing good behavior from them, while simultaneously providing the teens with work experience on one of the Temple's many community projects. More often than not, the teens would remain affiliated with the Temple long after they were required to do so. Other teenagers were sent to vocational school or college at Temple expense. And most of the children whose parents had joined the Temple and who were raised in the church remained after they themselves reached maturity.

Peoples Temple also operated the Peoples Restaurant, which reportedly fed over 1,700 meals each day to members who lived in communes around the city, as well as to the city's homeless people. There were free tutoring lessons, vocational classes, self-defense classes, and other activities aimed at various parts of the community. The Temple ran a kennel to care for local stray animals, and paid the rent of a pet adoption clinic when it was faced with eviction. With the Temple move to San Francisco, its political focus became more progressive. While in Indiana and Ukiah, Temple members pursued the church's teachings into the workplace, finding jobs in local and state agencies to assist the rural poor. After moving to San Francisco, though, the Temple created its own community-building programs, following its own ideological precepts and models.

Peoples Temple contributed money to a variety of progressive causes, including the American Civil Liberties Union, the National Association for the Advancement of Colored People, the Angela Davis Defense Fund, the American Indian Movement, and the United Farm Workers. It donated money to families of police officers killed in the line of duty. While based in Ukiah, the Temple saved the community $3,000 by painting the local elementary school. Community groups supported by the church were allowed to use Temple resources – including the Temple's printing press – free of charge.

All of the many community based services, as well as the daylong vibrant Temple meetings, contrasted greatly with the traditional San Francisco black churches of the time, giving people a spiritual outlet that was simply not being offered elsewhere. The Temple did direct outreach to segments of the community that had long been forgotten by the San Francisco establishment, both black and white. As the black church structure was described by Reverend J. Alfred Smith, "The 1970's were a dark age for the Black Church in San Francisco. Most churches had become little more than social clubs, where chicken dinners and raffle tickets were the only activities on the agenda. In these houses of worship, the red carpet in the church narthex became a fashion runway for the fur coat and Brooks Brothers suit crowd. After the Sunday morning service was finished, the church fathers would seal the buildings up tighter than Pharaoh Ramses' tomb."

People were drawn to the Temple for a variety of reasons: some people went because they needed help; some went to provide that help. Some were drawn to spiritual socialism, others went for the faith healings, and some just came to listen to the music. In addition to the professional quality of music from Loretta and Deanna, Peoples Temple was well known for its various musical groups. The African Dancers performed at a number of city events, as did the Soul Steppers, a dance and acrobatic group comprised of six Temple teens. The Peoples Temple gospel choir also produced a record, "He's Able." Most folks came to Peoples Temple and stayed for a multitude of reasons, basically because everything seemed to fit.

Garry Lambrev, Teresa King, Diane Lundquist

Things were not going well for Garry Lambrev, who had again left the Temple. His bisexual partner began a relationship with a woman named Teresa King. Teresa was a young woman from Texas, raised in Arizona, who had moved to the Bay Area and worked at Kepler's Bookstore in Menlo Park. She was fascinated by Garry's stories of a revolutionary interracial church located in the secluded Redwood Valley community. By 1974, they were looking to escape what Garry described as "mutually self-destructive relationships which we'd experienced with our unattached friend Gerry on the outside." When Garry returned to Peoples Temple, Teresa went with him.

Teresa's attraction to Jim Jones and Peoples Temple went beyond progressive politics. After joining the Temple and moving into a Temple commune, Teresa got devastating news that cancer had spread throughout her body and at the very young age of 26, she had a hysterectomy to remove all traces of the cancer. When she was with the Temple, she felt active, healthy and alive. While recovering from surgery, she was swarmed with loving affection from numerous Temple members, including Marceline Jones. After her recovery, she began working in the Temple's extensive library, cataloguing and organizing its thousands of books, many of them donated by Garry Lambrev.

Before making any decision to return to the Temple one last time, Garry ran into Temple attorney Tim Stoen at a rally on the steps of the San Francisco Federal building. Stoen warned him that the political circumstances within the Temple had changed radically since Garry had left. A multi-part exposé by Rev. Lester Kinsolving in *The San Francisco Examiner* in September 1972 had called the validity of the faith healings into question and the church was now much more sensitive to publicity. It also had assumed less patience for people coming and going. Garry had been allowed to come back several times in the past. Stoen made it clear that he would consider Gary to be a traitor if he left again.

Indeed, Temple life had changed quite drastically after the Kinsolving exposé. More and more people were encouraged to live communally and work exclusively for the Temple, and contact with outsiders and family members who had not joined was discouraged. Services were expanded to include more discipline: people were called to the front of the congregation and publicly ridiculed for violating a church infraction. The person was often forced to fight someone of superior strength or was beaten with a two-by-four, called the "board of education." Eventually this developed into public beatings and various other forms of humiliation. The Temple also adopted a reporting method through which people were expected to write down the details – names and circumstances – when other Temple members violated church rules. In a sense, the Temple had evolved into a network of spies and informants, increasing a sense of isolation for many members within a group of over two thousand other people.

> Like so much with the church the physical discipline began in a small way and only gradually reached extremes. It had started with a few light spankings for children. Then a paddle-like one-by-four inch 'Board of Education' was introduced. The paddling became more severe and was often administered by a rotund black woman named Ruby Carroll, who was chosen for her physical strength, not a mean disposition … The swats varied in number and intensity. Some were spanked almost half-heartedly, or in fairly good humor. Other spankings qualified as beatings …

Around this time, Alan Swanson got a call at the commune that an old member was returning and needed someone to sit with him. Alan was scheduled to be there at 3:00 am, but ended up sleeping through the shift. When he realized what happened, Alan looked for the new person to apologize. The returning member, Garry Lambrev, remembered the grueling Temple schedule, and understood why Alan was not able to make it. The two men became immediate friends.

Garry became accustomed to the changes he saw in the community.

He kept himself busy writing letters in the communications office, tutoring Temple children, and of course attending the various meetings and services.

Eventually Garry was assigned to the second-hand store, Relics-N-Things, which the Temple used to sell the items donated by members, when they joined the various communal homes. He created a little spot for himself there, working with two other members. One of the women Garry worked with was a biracial woman named Diane Lundquist. Diane's family lived in Berkeley, and her mother was a member of the Communist Party. It was natural that Diane, who was raised with the same interracial, anti-poverty views espoused by the church, would be attracted to the Temple. Her sister, Joan, also joined the church, and their mother often attended services. Garry introduced Teresa and Diane, and as the women got to know each other better, they developed a loving, supportive relationship.

Vern Gosney, Edith Cordell

Though the Temple moved its base to San Francisco, a number of members stayed in the Ukiah area including Cheryl and Vernon Gosney. Living in a Temple commune, Cheryl was now pregnant and expressed uncertainty of her new family's participation in the Temple. She had a falling out with a woman who had refused to compensate her for babysitting, and took her complaint to the church leadership. When the Temple sided with the other woman, Cheryl decided she was going to leave the church, and Vernon left with her.

A few months later, while giving birth to her son, Cheryl was overdosed with anesthetic and lapsed into an irreversible coma. Anxious about a pending lawsuit against the hospital, overwhelmed with the responsibility of Mark, the newborn baby, and unable to turn to his racist family members who disowned him for marrying a black woman, Vernon rejoined Peoples Temple and moved to San Francisco. Jones used this episode to emphasize to the rest of the congregation what would happen to them if they left his protection. Not only had Cheryl become very ill after questioning the Temple, but it seemed Vernon had acknowledged his family's errors by returning to the church following the tragedy. Vernon's suit against the hospital was eventually thrown out after the hospital argued it was unable to tell that Cheryl was turning blue from lack of oxygen because she was "too black." Though appalling by today's judicial standards, the decision spoke to the institutionalized racial climate in America of the time. It certainly convinced Vernon that his place was with the Temple.

As most Temple members did, Vernon allowed his son Mark to be raised by the collective Temple membership. Vernon held down a job, maintained the Temple's rigorous schedule, and spent time attending to his comatose wife, but felt Mark was not getting adequate care. Through the Temple services, he met Edith Cordell, who never married or had children of her own. Nevertheless, she raised twenty people from infancy to adulthood, though she was not always the legal guardian. She lived in a trailer which was always immaculately maintained, regardless of how many children she had in her care. Little Mark Gosney was soon placed with Edith Cordell, who accepted the biracial newborn as her own son. As had become the custom in Peoples Temple, Vernon lived communally and was responsible for helping to raise other members' children.

Alan Swanson

When the Temple's headquarters moved from Ukiah to San Francisco, Alan Swanson – like a number of other members – stayed in the Redwood Valley area. By this time he held down three jobs, bringing in a steady flow of money. Alan also preferred to work because it was one of the few acceptable reasons for missing meetings; he had grown increasingly uncomfortable with the new levels of discipline in the church. He enjoyed the community and loved the people, but no longer felt the meetings were positive experiences. Though he still had to attend some services, he let his job provide the opportunity to skip others or arrive late whenever he could.

At times Alan attended services in San Francisco, traveling from Ukiah in the convoy of Temple buses. As did most Temple members, Alan craved sleep. Because of overcrowded conditions, Alan volunteered to ride in the luggage compartments above the seats, so he could catch some sleep. During a few visits to the San Francisco church, Alan had the opportunity to go into the Castro. He would slip away on some errand and find himself at a local gay bar. He missed the camaraderie of the gay community but was satisfied with his little forbidden trips.

Eventually Alan was appointed as a guard captain to one of the Temple's various security teams and spent most of his time guarding the Ukiah or San Francisco churches. The highlight of guard duty at the Ukiah church was the Temple's pet chimp, Mr. Muggs, whose cage was under the guard tower. Even though the Temple told the public that the monkey was saved from a torturous life in a research laboratory, how the Temple actually obtained Mr. Muggs is unclear. The Temple used Mr. Muggs as a showpiece of opposition to vivisection, or the use of animals in scientific research.

Many of the residents of Ukiah had resented the intrusion of the interracial, politically active church into their community. One night, while

Alan was on guard duty, a group of teens drove by the guard tower, screamed obscenities, and threw a half-empty whiskey bottle at the church. Alan picked up the bottle and placed it next to the tower. When he finished his shift the next morning, he forgot to report the incident to his replacements, found who the bottle and immediately reported Alan for drinking on the job. Temple members were expected to abstain from alcohol, and Alan was called up on the floor at the following meeting and confronted with the whiskey bottle. When Alan finished explaining what had happened – that he was guilty of not reporting the incident but he had not been drinking – Jones told the congregation that Alan was telling the truth, that Alan would never drink. A bell went off inside Alan's head. Even though Alan was telling the truth in this instance, it was also true that occasionally he did slip away when in San Francisco to have a beer. If Jones was psychic, how could he not know this? He was also shocked that Jones had not discovered that Alan had been secretly saving money. The first seeds of doubt about Jones' omnipotence took root in Alan's mind.

Jones finished the session by telling Alan that he needed to join one of the Temple's communes. Alan spent some time thinking about Jones' request and knew it was time to commit or split. He decided to dedicate himself to the Temple, left his cottage, and moved in with a number of other young people from the Temple. He was still working three jobs and oftentimes found he was too tired to go to Temple functions. Occasionally he lied about when he had to work, and instead of going into a job, he would drive out into a secluded part of town and sleep in his car.

Linda Mertle, Cynthia Davis

Although Linda Mertle was young, she knew what she wanted, and she wanted Cynthia Davis. Cynthia was from rural Texas, where she had been raised by a superstitious mother who practiced a form of religion that was a cross between rural witchcraft and strict Catholicism. Cynthia's father, on the other hand, refused to attend church functions, often resulting in family disputes. Cynthia was bright and cheery and happily accompanied her mother on her initial trips to Peoples Temple. Cynthia's mother was attracted to the healing services and fervently believed in Jim Jones' paranormal, clairvoyant powers. Soon Cynthia, her brother, and their reluctant father were regularly attending Temple services with Cynthia's mother.

Linda noticed Cynthia from afar, and even though Cynthia was dating a man at the time, Linda slowly ingratiated herself into Cynthia's life. Linda simply asked Cynthia to break it off so that they could be together. Cynthia obliged and – despite nine years difference in age – she and Linda began dating and spending a lot of time together.

During a 1974 service in San Francisco, however, Linda saw Inez, a member who had not been coming to meetings in almost a year. Even though Linda knew she should not associate with people who had not attended meetings for such a long time, she had always had a crush on Inez. As Inez left the church, she gave Linda the eye, and Linda followed her out to the parking lot where they could have a private talk. The two women ducked between the parked buses where Linda immediately found herself in a passionate embrace. Despite her sincere affection for Cynthia, Linda felt an excitement she had never felt before, but it was not to last long.

One of the security guards had seen the two women slip out of the building and followed them to the parking lot. Ignoring Inez, the guard grabbed Linda by the collar and dragged her back inside the Temple. He brought her downstairs to the concession stand where her parents were working. Linda knew she was in trouble, knew she should not have left the service, and knew she should not have been caught with Inez, especially so intimately. When her father was faced with the truth that his little girl was in fact a lesbian, it was more than he could bear and he punched Linda in the face. Enraged, Linda balled up her fist and smacked her father back. It was a mistake. He unleashed on his daughter by beating her to the ground, hog-tying her and leaving her on the floor under a table for the night. And the punishment was only the beginning.

No one talked to Linda for the remainder of the week, and at the next weekly catharsis meeting, people avoided her eyes. At the members-only meeting in Ukiah, Jones summoned Linda to the floor. As Linda's stepmother, Jeannie Mills recalled:

> Our sixteen-year-old daughter Linda was called up for confrontation. She had hugged a girlfriend whom Jim considered to be a traitor. Linda stood before Jim and admitted that she was guilty. Jim looked at her sternly, 'You have been unwise, in the past, in your choice of friends, and it is important that we teach you a lesson you won't forget. Your only friends are to be the people who come to our services. Outsiders, or people who come when they feel like it, are not friends.'

Jones then sentenced Linda to 75 whacks with the "board of education," one of the most severe punishments to be meted out. One person lifted Linda by her legs, another person lifted her by her arms, and a rather large woman hit Linda with the board over and over as Jones laughingly kept count. Sometimes the board would not fall squarely, hitting her on her lower back or on her legs. But the most humiliating part of the whole ordeal was being forced to thank Jones after the beating. It is not clear why Jones sentenced Linda to such a severe punishment. Her father could have asked him, or her parents' status in the church leadership could have increased her punishment as a test of their loyalty. Temple historians have often used this incident to establish that Peoples Temple was anti-gay and Linda was beaten for being a lesbian. Nothing could be further from the truth. Although Linda's father was not happy she was a lesbian, her offense in Jones' eyes was clearly that she was associating with a "traitor."

A similar incident later in Jonestown, as documented by Edith Roller in a journal entry supports this conclusion: In a catharsis session, two boys who had been told to stay apart were on the floor for stealing items which they used to outfit a hideout for purposes of sexual experimentation. The boys were slow to confess what they had been doing, and even slower to admit that they took turns being on top. Jones took a casual attitude towards the sexual behavior which he said was natural, but he was severe about the stealing.

Linda was literally not able to sit down for days. When she went to school, other teens from the Temple crowded around her as she changed her clothes for physical education classes so that her teachers would not see the severe bruises which covered her backside for weeks. She was removed from her parents' home and placed for six months with Thelma Darnes who warned Linda that she had killed her first two husbands and would bury Linda in the back yard if she misbehaved. Linda toed the line, but occasionally stole away to see Cynthia when the Temple was in LA. When her six-month sentence with Thelma was up, Linda moved to a very small room in the San Francisco Temple where she was able to actively resume her relationship with Cynthia.

Jamie Gill

The only known transgendered person in Peoples Temple was a transsexual woman named Jamie Gill, who was from a large family with many members in the church. During a service in San Francisco, Jamie got up to go to the bathroom and was stopped by a guard because Temple members were required to stay in their seats for the duration of the services, especially during Jones' sermons. This particular time Jamie was not going to take no for an answer. She told the guard she was menstruating and needed to use the facilities. Her ruse, however, did not fool the streetwise guard, who recognized her as a transsexual and called her up on the floor for confrontation. Jamie was chastised for getting up during the service, but to the complete confusion of the entire congregation, stuck to her story about menstruating. The Temple leadership was at a loss as to what to do with her. Though she was let off with just a reprimand, Jamie came under closer scrutiny and was continually called up for confrontation. One evening Jamie's antics earned her the promise of a beating, but she saw it coming and slipped out of the Los Angeles Temple and disappeared into the night.

Although Jamie is the only transgendered member of Peoples Temple whom survivors could recall, transgendered people were mentioned in a promotional flier produced for the Jonestown community. Many versions of the flier were circulated, and a copy was reprinted in *The San Francisco Examiner* as a column entitled "Fresh start in the Jungle for the City's Misfits." The flier states: "They cut a road seven miles into the South American rain forest and then made a clearing. Today if you visit that clearing in the jungle, you will find a little band of misfits from the streets of San Francisco trying to start a new life. You'll find a purse snatcher feeding pigs, a shoplifter hoeing corn, a transvestite driving a tractor, a prostitute and a couple of dope addicts in the sewing shed making their own clothes." Today transsexuals are no longer viewed as social deviants, and the gay and lesbian community in San Francisco would not tolerate equating gender variance behavior with crime. Though there were transsexuals in Peoples Temple, Jonestown survivors could not recall a transsexual working on the heavy machinery in Jonestown. The inclusion of transsexuals in the flier, albeit in a backhanded way, could be considered outreach to and acceptance of the transgendered community.

Peoples Temple And The Gay Community

━━━━━━━━━━━━━━━━ ⌘ ━━━━━━━━━━━━━━━━

Once it settled into San Francisco, Peoples Temple began to focus its energies cultivating substantive, influential political clout throughout California. By 1976, three of San Francisco's top elected officials – Mayor George Moscone, District Attorney Joseph Freitas, and Sheriff Richard Hongisto – had the strong support of Jim Jones and the volunteer work of hundreds of Temple members. As a reward for his help in the election, Moscone appointed Jones to chair on the city's powerful Housing Commission. Temple support came to be considered so crucial that – as then-California Assemblyman Willie Brown remarked – "In a tight race, forget it without Jones."

One of the many politicians who came to the Temple was Harvey Milk, a gay East Coast transplant who moved into the Castro District and became involved in local politics. After failed campaigns for both the San Francisco Board of Supervisors and the California State Assembly, Harvey Milk won a seat on the Board of Supervisors in 1977. Milk is often mistakenly referred to as America's first openly gay elected official. That honor instead goes to Elaine Noble, who was a lesbian elected to the Massachusetts State Assembly in 1974, while the first elected gay man was Jim Yeadon, to the Madison, Wisconsin City Council in May 1977, after serving one term as an appointed member.

Harvey Milk was attracted to Peoples Temple for a number of reasons. Not only was support from the Temple pivotal in local elections, Milk was also drawn by the church's very public, pro-gay positions. Additionally, Milk recognized that the Temple was actively and effectively confronting the issues that were so important at the time: racism, poverty, war, and the ever-present specter of nuclear annihilation. Many Americans felt that nuclear war was inevitable. Coupled with this fear was a fundamental and widespread belief that individuals had the power to enact change, which was fueled by a newfound moral imperative to challenge the actions of their elected officials. Many people experimented with different living situations, and groups formed with varying structures from egalitarian communes to patriarchal-based families. Peoples Temple merged the two models. San Francisco especially nourished a leftist counterculture that confronted the establishment's approach to almost every problem facing the country, both foreign and domestic.

The gay and lesbian community in San Francisco was not immune to this wave of utopianism. As one letter writer to a San Francisco gay newspaper wrote in February 1976: "[T]hus the stage is set for potentially endless, violent conflicts (perhaps nuclear annihilation) as the poor 'have-nots' of the planet become increasingly aware, powerful and resistant to being bought off or co-opted by anything less than an equal share." Nothing is more indicative of the pervasive progressive bent on the gay community than the 1976 Gay Pride Parade instructions to contingents with floats: "No ageist, sexist, racist or classist displays, and any groups that spend more than $500 on a float are encouraged to match that amount in a donation to a gay and lesbian alcohol recovery program." Certainly a church that espoused a brand of progressive religious activism would have found fertile ground in San Francisco during the seventies. With its public support of gay and lesbian people, Peoples Temple was positioned to become that church. Indeed, there was much about the Peoples Temple philosophy that would have attracted gay- and lesbian-identified people, those seeking a spiritual outlet and/or those of a progressive persuasion.

The Temple focused on the congregation as family: Jim Jones evolved over time into "Father," and Marceline became "Mother." In adopting a socialist approach, the interracial congregation referred to each other as brothers and sisters. Creation of the congregation as a new family would be attractive, not only to people who had a negative family experience, but also for those who were looking to replace loved ones. Many gays and lesbians have difficulty coming out to their families, oftentimes resulting in irreparable damage. (This is not to perpetuate the idea that all queers have a hard time coming out to their families; however, especially in the seventies, many people came to San Francisco to escape the not-so-subtle homophobia which was just as much part of the American cultural fabric as racism, sexism and class bias.) The definition and focus on the congregation as family, with each member a brother and sister, as well as its attention to senior members, would have broad appeal to those searching for such stability, whether they were queer identified or not.

Peoples Temple publicly demanded support for gay people at a time that a majority of Americans were hostile to homosexuals. Almost every edition of *Peoples Forum,* the Temple's newspaper, which was delivered to most neighborhoods in San Francisco, carried a story about discrimination against gays and lesbians. The stories varied from exposés about police raids on gay bars and anti-gay police stings in public parks, to gay-bashing alerts and pieces about Nazi atrocities toward gays.

Despite the many pro-gay stories, *Peoples Forum* articles did not always receive the expected response. One gay letter writer of note, Jim Sherwood, responded to an article in the March 1977 edition about Jones' visit to Cuba. Jones had met with exiled Black Panther leader Huey Newton, who fled America to avoid trumped-up felony murder charges. Newton's parents were members of Peoples Temple, as was his cousin, Jonestown survivor Stanley Clayton. The *Peoples Forum* article reported Jones had talked to a number of Cubans about their living conditions, but had asked Newton about the quality of life for gays and lesbians in Cuba. Questioning the Panther's ability to speak on behalf of homosexuals, Sherwood took Jones to task for asking Newton about gay issues instead of demanding to speak directly to gays and lesbians themselves. And challenged the *Peoples Forum* spin that life for gays was terrible in America and great in Cuba: "Persecution of gay people in Cuba seems to be a fact. I'd say that one ought to criticize injustice everywhere, not just in America."

Another article of note in the March 1977 edition of *Peoples Forum* described the acceptance in Guyana of a bisexual actress. The piece is really a promotion piece for Guyana, especially the openness of the Guyanese, but it is also indicative of the importance, at least rhetorically, that Peoples Temple philosophically placed on the acceptance of sexual minorities. That one of the most widely circulated newspapers in San Francisco would write such controversial stories had to appeal to its queer readership, and certainly did not go unnoticed in the gay press.

Thomas Edwards, a well known gay conservative columnist, wrote in the March 24, 1977 edition of the gay newspaper, the *Sentinel,* that the staff of *Peoples Forum* was "comprised of revolutionary militants, terrorists and persons of radical philosophy" who were responsible for the election of Mayor George Moscone – the bane of conservatives – as well as District Attorney Joe Freitas and Sheriff Richard Hongisto. Edwards' column, "On the Right," ran opposite another column, "From the Left," occasionally written by Harvey Milk. The following edition's "From the Left" column by Randy Alfred responded to Edwards' assertion: "Here in San Francisco, the Peoples Temple, under the leadership of Jim Jones, is a fine example of a group understanding that freedom is truly indivisible. Peoples Temple, predominantly Black, has joined the Florida citrus boycott and intends to send a delegation to the Gay Freedom Day Parade. This group knows fascism must be fought not only in

Chile but right here, in our daily lives." Peoples Temple spokesperson Michael Prokes also criticized Edwards' column, leading *Sentinel* editors to reply: "The *Peoples Forum* recently carried an excellent article on the Nazi extermination of gay people. The *Sentinel* strongly supports the efforts of groups such as Peoples Temple to develop solidarity in San Francisco."

Not only did Peoples Temple send a delegation to the 1977 gay pride parade, they also had a member speak at the rally after the parade. The official schedule for the parade day listed ten speakers, including a speech by Mike Prokes titled "Straight Support for Gay People", along with well-known San Francisco activist Margo St. James.

Peoples Temple involvement in the Florida citrus boycott was no small act. By the late seventies, a number of ordinances protecting the rights of gays and lesbians from discrimination in employment and housing had been passed in various communities. In Dade County, Florida, however, former Miss America Anita Bryant launched a counter campaign, titled Save Our Children, to repeal the pro-gay ordinances. Using the basest stereotypes of the "gay predator," Bryant's forces successfully overturned the ordinance on June 7, 1977. Bolstered by a seven-to-three margin, the conservative forces immediately began promoting similar initiatives around the country. Soon, laws banning anti-gay discrimination were repealed in Eugene, Oregon; St. Paul, Minnesota; and Wichita, Kansas. In California, the effort manifested in the form of the Briggs initiative, Proposition Six, which would have prohibited people open about their homosexuality from being employed as teachers in the public school system. Gay men and lesbians around the country mobilized, targeting advertisers who used Bryant as a spokes model, specifically the Florida Citrus Commission. Gay bars around the country dumped Florida orange juice in favor of California's brands, while civic and church leaders lined up to purchase it.

Despite the fact that many churches remained silent on the issue; a large number of evangelical churches supported the anti-gay ballot measure. Peoples Temple, on the other hand, came out strongly in support of gay and lesbian Americans. Not only did the membership of the Temple take up a donation for the Dade County Coalition formed to oppose Bryant's efforts in Florida, but Jim Jones also sat as a member of the San Francisco-based Ad Hoc Committee to Support the Dade County Coalition. And in a lively display of pro-gay support, Peoples Temple publicly endorsed the boycott.

> Gay activist Howard Wallace, who was an organizer of the ad hoc
> group supporting the boycott, addressed a predominately Black
> church, the Peoples Temple, and received a rousing ovation from
> the several thousands attending when he asked their support
> in observing the boycott. The congregation voted to urge their

followers to participate in the boycott through an article in the church's newspaper, the *Peoples Forum*, which distributes 600,000 copies in the bay area weekly. The church congregation also voted with a standing, cheering vote to write their friends and relatives in the Miami area and asked them to observe the boycott.

In April 1977, Prokes read a statement from Jim Jones at a protest in the heavily gay Castro District in support of gay men and lesbians living in Dade County:

This vicious attack on the gay community by Anita Bryant is another sign of which way the wind is blowing – it's coming from the right and it's getting stronger. This marriage of pseudo-Christian morality and patriotism, backed up by corporate money, is giving birth to a new wave of fascism, and it's spreading its poison in attacking anything that's not straight white and conservative.

I think we ought to take a good look around us and a good look around our communities. Find out who among us is trying to cause division, trying to tear down unity, trying to call names and sow hatred.

We are entering a period where the rights of all minorities are going to be under attack even as we are attempting to emerge into full equality. There is a reactionary mood in middle America; and if the economic conditions worsen, as no doubt will happen according to all forecasts, we will be the scapegoats, we will be blamed – poor people, blacks, browns, gays, disabled people, everyone who doesn't fit into the 'right' mold, because the Anita Bryants are everywhere.

The fight against the anti-gay hate campaign is not just the fight of the gay community, but of all people who are endangered by this fascist mentality that hides behind beauty contest queens, pseudo religious revival, patriotic organizations, and the like. We all have a stake in this fight. I'm afraid that if we don't get together and present a united front, and forget small differences, we will be in danger of a new wave of fascist-like repression in the coming years, a nightmare that could mean the kind of insanity we're seeing in various nations like Chile, Iran and Argentina.

Let our theme be solidarity and let us build a coalition that will stand up to the reactionaries wherever and whenever they dare to oppress us!

Prokes went on to make the gay press with his own speech in which he said, if Anita Bryant "prays to a God that recognizes her insidious campaign against gay people, I don't want any part of him or it." This kind of overt support for the gay community, at a time when a number of religious groups were either leading the attack against gays or remaining silent, was unparalleled in the non-gay religious community. It was this unwavering support for gays that earned the loyalty of a number of people in the city's gay community. Reporters from around the country contacted Peoples Temple concerning its nontraditional approach in supporting gay people. In addition to Wallace, the Temple's political support for homosexuals also attracted the attention of gay teacher organizer Hank Wilson and gay political leader Harvey Milk.

Peoples Temple did receive some support for its opposition to the Bryant campaign and for defending the rights of gay men and lesbians in general. A letter to the *Peoples Forum* from the headquarters of the Black Panther Party drew the connections between racism and bigotry against homosexuals:

The Black Panther Party wishes to point out that shouting 'Faggot' while ruthlessly stabbing a gay human being several times, closely parallels this country's historical pattern of shouting 'nigger' while lynching, raping, or castrating a Black victim.

The whole human, multi-ethnic community – Black and poor people, homosexual and heterosexual alike – are victimized by the climate of fear and violence created by the Anita Bryants and John Briggses, those ultimately disposable types acting as front men or puppets for the powerful conservative interests which seek to stop social change in all areas.

They seek to open up a Pandora's Box of hysteria and hatred to drive back the people's movement for the human right to live a decent and fulfilling life.

This is the issue here: the human and civil rights of People, regardless of race or, indeed, sexual preference, to live out their lives free of bias and discrimination, free of racism and oppression, in order to develop to their full human potential.

The hidden dangers, the lies, and the potential for violence created by Anita Bryant's crusade in Florida ought now to be clear to us all. Just as she used the Bible to whip up a national backlash of unfounded fears and open hostility against gay people, so, too, was the Bible used for centuries to justify the enslavement of Blacks. Bigoted, racist minds need not be pushed too hard, need not be encouraged to attack innocent victims. America has taught Black people that lesson already.

Peoples Temple also publicly endorsed gay marriages by supporting the efforts of Anthony Sullivan and Richard Adams to have their relationship recognized by the federal government. On April 21, 1975, Sullivan and Adams were legally married in Boulder, Colorado, by gay Deputy County Clerk, Patrick Prince, after hearing that Prince had married a half dozen same-sex couples over a month's time without any action taken to stop him. Armed with the coveted marriage license, Adams then petitioned the Immigration and Naturalization Service (INS) to allow Sullivan, a citizen of Australia, to be allowed to live in the US as Adams' spouse.

The case was historically significant for gay people, because it challenged both the definition of marriage, as well as a 1965 law that banned immigration of homosexuals, under the exclusion of sexual deviant's clause (which would not be repealed until 1990). Already facing blistering hatred from the general public, Adams and Sullivan were still surprised by the level of bigotry from the INS, which responded to their petition by stating, "You have failed to establish that a bona fide marital relationship can exist between two faggots." A further complication was that – according to INS regulations – Adams and Sullivan had to declare their relationship had been consummated, an act that was illegal at the time. Fearing further public backlash, leaders in the gay community distanced themselves from the couple's efforts at federal recognition. Peoples Temple, however, not only publicly supported the efforts of Adams and Sullivan, it also made a "generous" donation to their defense fund. Adams and Sullivan's petitions were eventually denied after an extended battle with the federal government that spanned a decade and ended at the Supreme Court. The courts never nullified their marriage, but rather decided that the federal definition of marriage as being between a man and a woman overrode Colorado's marriage license. Richard Adams and Anthony Sullivan, who met in 1971, left the US when their appeals were exhausted; moving to

England and eventually settling in Australia. The gay community joined them in celebrating their 25th anniversary in 1996.

Jim Jones used Temple support for gays and lesbians for his own political gain whenever he could, most notably to reinforce a relationship with presidential candidate Jimmy Carter. The relationship had been initiated by Carter's sister Ruth Stapleton, who had become aware of Jones' faith healing services. In June 1976, Jimmy Carter's son, Chip, attended an annual fundraiser for the Guide Dogs for the Blind organization at the Mint Bar, a well-known gay establishment in San Francisco. The press ridiculed the future president's son, but Jones and Peoples Temple were quick to support him. In a taped phone conversation, Jones told Jimmy Carter's wife, Rosalyn, "There'd been some negative press about your son participating in raising funds for a gay bar, and I wanted to let you know we are one hundred percent behind you in that." While many political and religious leaders used the incident to attack Carter, or remained silent on the issue altogether, Peoples Temple was again on the forefront publicly supporting gay and lesbian issues.

An indication of the Peoples Temple influence on the gay and lesbian community is best illustrated by a letter sent to Jim Jones by gay community member Michael Delaney who, coincidently, represented the Harry S. Truman Democratic Club with Chip Carter at the Mint Bar fundraiser. As Delaney wrote:

> I just wanted you to know that I admire your good work here in San Francisco. Although I have never met you or even seen you, I feel as if I already knew you … As a gay man; I can sympathize with other minority groups more than ever. I, too, feel their oppression – the sting of bigotry, the dull oppression of ignorance. Because you have vibrated and acted so righteously against the dark sea of ignorance and bigotry that pervades this world – I believe you fulfill the role of a 20th Century prophet.

All of this without even meeting Jim Jones; Delaney's reaction was not unique.

After his first meeting at Peoples Temple, gay teacher Hank Wilson went home and wrote down the names and numbers of ten gay groups and more than forty gay and lesbian contact people who "demonstrated a Peoples Temple consciousness" including well known gay figures Pat Norman, Tom Ammiano, Randy Alfred and Randy Burns.

Even the local African American newspaper, *The Sun-Reporter*, commented on the support the Temple enjoyed from the gay and lesbian community. "Gay leaders Harvey Milk and Harvey Wallace both voiced support [for Jim Jones and Peoples Temple]. Wallace, head of Gay action, told the congregation,

'Peoples Temple has sent shock waves through the gay community. Rev. Jones has set an example for everybody who believes in human rights. Great numbers of gay people are well aware of your stand, and we won't forget it."

Despite its many pro-gay stances, Peoples Temple's philosophical approach to gay men and lesbians was outright contradictory. For example, as a loyalty test to Jim Jones, Temple members signed letters confessing to a variety of crimes. For many of these members, the crime which they confessed was to be a homosexual. One "Dear Dad" letter recovered in Jonestown confesses to membership in the radical Symbionese Liberation Army by a Jonestown resident who says he participated in bank robberies, kidnappings and murder; a second letter speaks of raping a little girl, cutting up her body and hiding it in the woods; next to these two is a note from a man extolling the pleasures of gay sex with a new partner who "fulfills all of my sexual needs."

Any group that has its members "admit" or "confess" homosexuality could hardly be called gay affirming; even though the congregation identified collectively as gay, and had a very pro-gay public persona. Jones clearly made a distinction by not identifying as gay himself. In this way he is separated from his congregation, holding heterosexuality as the highest standard, and recognizing that being a gay man or lesbian was simply part of being human. But it is still framed as an impurity. Again this is not very affirming for gay people.

Harvey Milk

Contrary to the popular myth that Harvey Milk's election was due to emerging gay political clout, Milk actually bucked the established gay leadership to launch his many campaigns. Political gay men and lesbians in the mid-seventies accepted that they had no chance of being elected; therefore it was prudent to throw gay support, specifically large financial contributions, behind gay-friendly candidates rather than gay candidates themselves. Milk's abrasive East Coast style only served to further alienate the low key San Francisco gay leadership.

Finding himself at odds with the gay leaders, Milk looked outside his community for support. He campaigned on a platform that was pro-people and could draw diverse crowds; he championed poor people and the senior citizens of the community, networked with senior political groups, made historic inroads with the labor movement, and initiated an alliance with Chinese political organizations. Because Milk was instrumental in getting the gay bars in San Francisco to join the labor-sponsored boycott of Coors Beer, a number of labor groups, including the Fireman's Union, the Teamsters, and the impressive Building and Construction Trade Council, all endorsed an openly gay man for elected office for the first time.

With his broad outreach, the young populist Milk soon came to the attention of the politically astute Jim Jones. Contacting Milk in 1976 during Milk's unsuccessful bid for a State Assembly seat, Jones offered to canvass the Haight Street area, despite the fact that he had already endorsed Milk's opponent Art Agnos. No matter who won the election, Jones had made sure the Temple would be on the winning side. Temple aide Sharon Amos was designated as liaison between the Temple and Milk, and the Milk campaign purchased a printing press for the surprisingly low sum of $200 from the Temple to print its campaign literature.

Milk's first trip to Peoples Temple was a campaign stopover that turned personal. Milk must have felt new-found importance as he was in the company of a number of prominent San Francisco personalities including Angela Davis and Art Agnos. When Milk returned home, he wrote a thank you note directly to Jim Jones. Dated Sunday March 22, 1976, Milk wrote that he was at the Temple to campaign, but while there, he found something more spiritual. He regretted having to leave the service early, despite being there for over four hours, but felt "a high" long after leaving the church. Moved by an entire congregation which shared his political views, as well as by the warm reception, Milk added: "The life of a 'politician' is not one that gives you the chance to stay in a situation that you enjoy, for you must push on to other events – but, I found something dear today. I found a sense of being that makes up for all the hours and energy placed in a fight. I found what you wanted me to find. I shall be back, for I can never leave." This reveals the true emotion, the "high" many people felt after they left a Temple service. The letter is very personal, and though written in a political context, it is an indicator that Harvey Milk liked what he found at Peoples Temple and, after years of a semi-religious life, may have begun to feel real spiritual fulfillment at the socialist church.

Whether motivated spiritually, for political gain, or a combination of both, Harvey Milk returned many times to Peoples Temple. In the April 2, 1976 edition of *Peoples Forum*, Milk was listed along with a number of prominent people in support of Dennis Banks, the embattled American Indian Movement member who had close ties to Peoples Temple. In a letter dated April 27, 1976, Milk expresses his gratitude for being mentioned in the latest edition of the Temple newspaper. Milk also thanks Jones for the Temple's support in his campaign for State Assembly; the success of which Milk feels incredibly optimistic. A photo of Milk speaking at the podium of Peoples Temple also appears on the cover of the August 1977 issue, along with a number of other San Francisco politicians who attended a service in support of Jim Jones and his church.

Milk's next letter to Jones dated December 12, 1976, comments on the new format of *Peoples Forum*. It also laments the state of America and ponders if the political situation will ever get better. The letter then moves on to a more personal tone: "Our paths [sic] have crossed. They will stay crossed. It is a fight that I will walk with you into. Whenever I seem to get a little low I seem to get a copy of the *Peoples Forum*. It gives me the strength to wake up and realize that one cannot get tired. There is no time for that. I shall not get tired." Milk's relationship with the Temple evolved over time, reflecting not only a political alliance, but also a spiritual connection. Milk gave the Temple credit for his ability to continue his political fights and reaffirmed his solidarity with the progressive church. To drive the point home, Milk emphasized his support for Jim Jones and Peoples Temple by pledging: "The first time I heard you, you made a statement: 'Take one of us and you must take all of us.' Please add my name."

One of Milk's many accomplishments was founding the Castro Street Fair. Originally an afternoon for local merchants to showcase their wares, today the Castro Street Fair has turned into a weekend celebration with artisans from around the world and a crowd that numbers into the hundreds of thousands. Many people were critical of Milk's plans, accusing him of just trying to boost the local economy, and in turn, his little camera store on Castro Street. But Milk was determined to have a good showing, so in addition to the food booths, artisan displays, and vending merchants, Milk organized speeches from a central stage. For entertainment, he asked his friends from Peoples Temple to come and perform, and a troupe of Temple teens sang and danced for the overflow Castro crowd. A note sent to the church from Milk, thanking the teens for their wonderful performance, is located in the Temple archives.

The last note which Harvey Milk is known to have written to Jim Jones comes from the spring of 1977. It refers to what must have been one of Jones' last speeches in San Francisco and again has a more personal than political tone: "Jim – Hearing your voice Sunday gave me a warm feeling – I'm so glad that the ear trouble has not lowered your ability to fight and to fight so greatly – my name is cut into stone in support of you and your people."

Milk aide Danny Nicolletta accompanied Milk on this visit to Peoples Temple. Nicolletta recalled seeing people he identified as gay, an observation corroborated by gay Temple member Vernon Gosney, who stated that the Temple leadership would have strategically placed gay people around Milk and his friends. Nicolletta confessed he was excited after the Temple service, but that Milk warned him not to be taken in by Peoples Temple. Nicolletta thought Milk admired Jim Jones, and might have even looked to him as an equal, but he would never have become involved in the Jones persona-based church. Milk was a leader, not a follower; he may have been envious of Jones' leadership skills, but he was too clever, or egotistical, to be taken in himself.

Nicolletta recalled when he went to use the restroom in the middle of the multi-hour service, a guard accompanied him. He had never been to a church with guards before, nor had he ever been escorted to the bathroom. To him the whole experience felt a bit creepy, but it did not draw away from his excitement about the overall trip to the church. As Milk and his group left, members of the Temple security team walked them to their car. This may have been because the church was located in a tough neighborhood, and it would not help to have visiting dignitaries mugged on their way to or from the church.

Not many people had a direct line to Harvey Milk. Reporter Bill Barnes of the *San Francisco Examiner* was one of them; Marceline and Jim Jones were two others. Nicolletta confirmed that Milk let calls from Jones or his wife Marceline be sent directly through to him. Nicolletta stated that the calls mostly came from Marceline Jones and usually involved upcoming Temple events.

According to Milk's biographer Randy Shilts, when Milk aide Anne Kronenberg asked Harvey about the volunteers from Peoples Temple, he responded, "They're weird but excellent volunteers. You take help where it comes from but don't trust them." This attitude of Milk toward the Temple is reinforced in *Stitching a Revolution,* by former Milk staffer Cleve Jones. According to Jones, Milk was close enough to Peoples Temple that when he wanted a good turnout for a press conference, he called the Temple, and the church would send over a busload of people at the prearranged time. It is not clear how often Milk contacted the Temple for members, but it must have been quite often, considering his reputation for drawing large diverse crowds. Cleve Jones' quote of Milk after the press conference regarding the Temple assistance is almost identical to Shilts': "They were weird but excellent volunteers. You take help where it comes from, but don't trust them."

Ruling out plagiarism, the similarities of the comments could only indicate that Milk's feelings about Peoples Temple were emphatic and heartfelt. But former Temple member Garry Lambrev acknowledged the underlying belief: "I am sure it was common knowledge among San Francisco politicians of the era, particularly those supported by [Jim] Jones, that his followers were 'weird', i.e. not the supporters you would expect to follow the campaign trail, but rather poor, relatively uneducated who did what they were told." Still most politicians graciously accepted the Temple volunteers, whether they were weird or not.

Harvey Milk lost the 1976 California Assembly bid by a few thousand votes, a good showing for a virtually unknown candidate running against one of the most popular politicians from the San Francisco Bay Area. He could not have achieved such a feat if it were not for the help from Peoples Temple. Milk remained in politics, and in 1977 he was elected to the San Francisco Board of Supervisors. With personal interests and support, Harvey Milk would share personal bonds and political connections with Jim Jones and Peoples Temple until the end of their lives.

Nowhere in Harvey Milk's archives, either at the California Historical Society or the San Francisco Public Library, are there letters from the Temple leadership responding to the supervisor's correspondence, though the library does house over fifty letters sent to Milk from the residents of Jonestown when Milk's lover, Jack Lira, committed suicide in September 1978. Temple members were prolific writers, and it's difficult to believe that they would not have responded to any of Milk's letters, especially as he became more popular and politically influential. Traditionally the Temple would have sent Milk prayer clothes, photos of Jones and fund-raising letters, in addition to any specific responses to his letters. It is suspicious that none of these things appear in Milk's personal or private effects.

THE ALLEGATIONS

$$\boxplus$$

Garry Lambrev, Alan Swanson

Garry Lambrev stayed with the Temple until 1976, but grew increasingly concerned about the changes within the church. The spying, beatings, and overall paranoia that pervaded the church became too much for him to handle. As the Temple grew, it morphed from a communal utopian paradise in the lush Redwood Valley to a militant urban socialist outpost.

Despite its numerous good works, Peoples Temple faced another public relations crisis in 1977, reminiscent of the Lester Kinsolving articles of five years earlier. Former members – considered traitors or defectors by the general Temple membership – came forward with allegations against the church leadership ranging from property theft, assault, fraud, child abuse, brainwashing and even murder. People outside the Temple who had worked on campaigns that lost to political candidates and issues endorsed by Jim Jones, seized on the opportunity to discredit the progressive church.

No one escaped the wrath of meetings, and in January 1976, Garry was called up before the congregation on the pretext of a suspected sexual liaison with Alan Swanson. But there was a problem. Yes, they were both gay, good friends and roommates but – even if no one in the Temple believed them – they had not had sex. Neither of the accused men offered a defense for fear of receiving a beating, but the confrontation left Garry feeling more angry than humiliated.

He was also profoundly confused. Until then he had every reason to believe in Jones' paranormal gifts. Now he saw that Jones, the man he thought was the living God, could be wrong. And if Jones was wrong about him and Alan having a sexual relationship, what else could he be wrong about?

And if he doubted Jim Jones, what did that mean about the Temple itself? Still, it was not easy for him to decide to leave. He had found peace and was comfortable in his busy routine, surrounded by friends and family devoted to a common cause.

In August 1976, Garry tried to convince his closest friend, Liz Foreman, to return to the Temple. Liz, the daughter of Julius Epstein, a well-known movie director blacklisted during the McCarthy years, had recently defected from the group and was hiding out across the Bay. Garry's attempt to get her to return to the Temple backfired: she talked him into leaving. As they compared notes, they realized Jim Jones was more human than God, and the violent discipline in the church was only getting worse.

A number of incidents also led them to question the evolving direction of the church. The first incident was the humiliation of a young woman in the Temple who was ordered to stand before the Planning Commission and stripped of her clothing as Jones and other members ridiculed her. Unlike other punishments in the Temple, the purpose of this act seemed like nothing more than humiliation and embarrassment, as the woman had not done anything to warrant such cruel treatment. In fact, she was one of Jones' most loyal and dedicated followers.

The Temple leadership had also overseen the severe beating of Peter Wotherspoon, a close friend of Alan, Garry and Liz. Peter was a pedophile and had been caught molesting Temple boys *and* girls. Jones did not want to call the authorities and felt the best way to handle the situation was to beat Peter so severely that he would never think of touching another boy again. Peter was beaten until he passed out, was resuscitated and then beaten unconscious again. Even by Temple standards, it was a brutal beating. Analyzing it much like Linda Mertle's beating, many Temple historians have written that Peter was beaten for being gay. Upon closer inspection it is clear this is not the case. The Temple leadership struggled with the appropriate punishment, including turning Peter over to the police. They also tried to find Peter a suitable male companion. But Peter had no interest in a relationship with an adult gay male and preferred to stay with his wife Mary.

Although Garry and Alan knew Peter had molested the children, they felt the punishment was too severe. If pedophilia was a sickness, was it appropriate to beat a sick person? How was this really helping Peter? Were there other, less violent ways to ensure the safety of the Temple children? These questions were not asked, much less answered, in the mob mentality that lead to the violent frenzy surrounding Peter's beating. For Garry, though, the incident was enough to convince him, it was again time to leave.

In the company of Liz Foreman, Garry arrived late one night at Relics-N-Things to quickly gather a few of his possessions while everyone in the tiny commune was groggy with sleep. They had to turn on a light in order to pack his bags. The disturbance aroused the manager, Bev Livingston, who placed a call to central headquarters a mile away. As Garry and Liz pulled away, they saw Jim Jones' adopted Asian son, Lew, and top Temple lieutenant, Maria Katsaris, drive up. After a citywide chase that lasted the better part of an hour, Liz and Garry lost their pursuers between San Francisco's Chinatown and North Beach.

Once Garry got settled in his hiding place, he called the Temple to arrange the picking up of the rest of his things. Jones got on the phone and used a "carrot and stick" to convince him to stay with the church. After a prolonged argument, Garry told Jones he no longer felt Jones was God, and that if he were God, he was misusing his power. He could not get around the fact that Jones had accused him of acts he had never done, nor could he find justification for the brutal treatment of Linda and Peter, and the humiliation of the young woman. The magic was gone. There was no going back. In a final act of power, he hung up on Jim Jones, symbolically cutting the ties with his God forever.

As he arranged to do, Garry contacted the Temple a half hour before retrieving his remaining personal effects. He was met at the store by a Temple security team, led by Jim McElvane, a large man who stood six foot, seven inches tall. He handed Garry his lockbox, now unlocked of course, a jumble of papers obviously searched. His personal writings were intact but his passport and community college teaching credential were gone.

Whenever Alan Swanson had a problem with the direction of the Temple, he thought it was just him, and that he was being self-indulgent, but the discipline had become too severe. Once he saw a woman's hands tied behind her back as she was thrown into the Temple's swimming pool, which was often used for mass baptisms. Alan realized the woman was in real danger of dying, if not from drowning, then from sheer panic. He did not want to have a similar experience and felt for the first time that he did not even want to be part of the discipline. It was becoming too much for him.

Alan got a call from an old friend in San Francisco who had driven to Ukiah. Alan knew he was supposed to hang around only with members from the Temple, but he really enjoyed his friend's time and decided it would not be too bad to go to a movie. As they were waiting in line, Alan noticed a group of Temple members, including an associate pastor, Jack Beam, further up the line. Alan could not believe his eyes. The thought that Temple insiders, the most pious of the group, would flaunt Temple rules was shocking to him. He began to wonder how a group of Temple members could go to the movies together and not worry about any of the others reporting the trip. How often did they do it, and where did they get the money for the tickets? Like many members of Peoples Temple, Alan had a life outside the group, but he never expected that other people did too, especially people in leadership positions who were supposed to set an example.

Alan tried to process all of these new emotions. He was becoming disillusioned with the church and was not sure what to do, when he and Garry Lambrev were called up and confronted about their non-existent relationship. Alan already had doubts about Jones being the living God, ever since the incident with the whiskey bottle. He knew it was only a matter of time before he would leave the Temple. When his mother in Wisconsin became sick, he got permission to return home to help take care of her. While there, he received a number of letters from Temple members offering words of encouragement and support. Alan stayed home longer than expected, and his feelings about leaving the Temple changed from time to time.

As Alan made plans to return to Ukiah, Garry called to tell him that their friend, Liz Foreman, had left the church. Garry explained to Alan that he was going to call Liz to persuade her to return to the Temple, and was wondering if Alan had heard from her. Alan replied he had not, and asked Garry to keep him posted. A few nights later, both Garry and Liz called Alan to tell him that Garry also left the church. They also told Alan about the beating of their friend, Peter Wotherspoon. The two friends now wanted to convince Alan either to remain in Wisconsin or to stay with them in Ukiah, but not to return to Peoples Temple. Alan decided to return to Ukiah, but Garry and Liz met him at the airport and took him to where they were hiding.

During the weekend, when they knew most of the Temple members would be in San Francisco or Los Angeles, Alan and Garry sneaked back to the commune where Alan had left his things during his time in Wisconsin. They entered the residence to find all of Alan's possessions had been removed. Most likely someone from the Temple had called Alan's home in Wisconsin and found out he had already left, and they removed everything he owned from the commune. The two men then went to the lot where the buses and cars were kept. The buses were gone, of course, but Alan's car was still there. Usually Temple members turned the title of their cars over to the Temple; the members were allowed the use of the cars, but the Temple actually owned them. Once they turned in their car's title, members could have their cars repaired or tuned up at the Temple's machine shop. But Alan had never surrendered his title. Garry and Alan opened the gate, and Alan used his spare key to repossess his car.

One of the most influential people to defect from Peoples Temple was Grace Stoen, wife of then-San Francisco Assistant District Attorney, Tim Stoen. The Stoens had been members of the Temple's inner circle since the early seventies. Complicating this defection of a top lieutenant was the issue of the paternity of Grace Stoen's son, John Victor Stoen. Both Stoens had signed sworn affidavits attributing paternity to Jim Jones; however the credibility of the statements was questionable, as Temple members often signed false affidavits as loyalty tests. At the same time, Grace Stoen never denied having a sexual relationship with Jim Jones prior to conception, nor was Jones known to have had other people sign similar paternity documents. Almost a year after Grace's defection in July 1976, Tim also left the church and immediately joined his estranged wife in her attempts to retrieve the child they had left in Jones' custody.

In addition to the potentially embarrassing paternity suit, a number of news articles appeared examining the Temple's role in 1976 San Francisco elections, with allegations of voter registration fraud and theft. On August 1, 1977, *New West* Magazine published an article in which ten Temple defectors told their stories of what went on "inside" Peoples Temple. Adding spice to the publication was the claim by *New West*'s editors that Temple members had broken into their offices in an attempt to discover the contents of the upcoming exposé and to intimidate the magazine into canceling the story. They notified the police that the only thing in their office that had been disturbed was the folder on Peoples Temple. From the start of their investigation, though, the police questioned the veracity of the alleged break-in and determined that a *New West* employee had broken in after having locked himself out of the building earlier in the week. With this information, the report of the tampered Temple file was seen to be wishful thinking. However, the magazine editors never retracted the allegation, and the negative press associated with the "break-in," coupled with the pending paternity suit, convinced Jones to send five-year-old John Victor Stoen to Jonestown, beyond the reach of the American judicial system. The Temple also began to accelerate the migration of its members to its agricultural mission in Jonestown, culminating in a mass exodus of almost a thousand people to the remote jungle outpost by the fall of 1977, and leaving only a few hundred members in San Francisco and Ukiah to manage its stateside financial and business affairs. Jones himself arrived in Jonestown in August 1977, never again to leave the community bearing his name.

Harvey Milk

The Temple leadership also responded to the negative press of the summer of 1977 by asking a number of prominent politicians to rally to their cause. In his defense of Peoples Temple, Harvey Milk wrote to *New West* that: Jones "posses [possesses] as much integrity as anyone I've ever met."

Milk also joined other well-known politicians, including California Lieutenant Governor Mervyn Dymally, San Francisco Mayor George Moscone, and State Assemblyman Willie Brown in writing to Forbes Burnham, the Prime Minister of Guyana, in support of Peoples Temple. Milk's letter of August 5, 1977, goes to great lengths to defend the church, albeit in a somewhat rambling way: "The good I see. The good I hear. The work that Peoples Temple does for my community and the good that Peoples Temple does for other communities. Communities like mine at every aspect must be considered communities that have been passed over by our so-called democracy. If other church's [churches] believed in Christianity like Peoples Temple does – if other people believed in democracy like Peoples Temple does then mankind in this nation would not be in the everlasting struggle it finds itself engaged in." Milk concludes his letter with unequivocal support for both the works and politics of Peoples Temple: "When those who do good are pointed at let it be pointed at for the good that they do. If that happens more people will be pointing at Peoples Temple then [than] at any other church in my community."

Giving credence to reports of an organized effort coordinated by the Temple, Howard Wallace's letter of support to Burnham was written on the same day as Milk's. The Temple quoted Wallace's letter in a widely-circulated promotional flier: "They [Peoples Temple] are now an object of right-wing attacks because they practice what they preach – solidarity with the oppressed and exploited of the earth. The Temple's consistent struggle on behalf of democratic rights and against social and economic inequality is without parallel, even in San Francisco, historically a center of progressive movements. I am one of many thousands in this city who take pride in counting Rev. Jim Jones and Peoples Temple among my friends."

The battle lines had been drawn. Peoples Temple and their prominent supporters were on one side, and former Temple members – including Tim and Grace Stoen, and Linda Mertle's parents who now called themselves Jeannie and Al Mills – and several relatives of Jonestown residents such as Steven Katsaris, the father of Jones confidante Maria Katsaris were on the other. The relatives formed a group that came to be called the Concerned Relatives. They began to circulate petitions, organize press conferences, and hold protests in front of the Temple's headquarters.

After the flurry of media stories concerning the *New West* article and the Temple's high profile responses, the two sides found themselves at an impasse. The Concerned Relatives group had no contact with the residents of Jonestown, much less the ability to retrieve their family members who lived there, whereas Jim Jones found he could not return from Guyana for fear of being arrested on charges of kidnapping John Victor Stoen. The

Concerned Relatives modified their strategy and began to file numerous complaints against the Temple with various government agencies. In one of these allegations, the relatives charged that from forty to sixty thousand dollars of Social Security checks were deposited every month into the church's coffers, while the intended recipients of the checks received inadequate food and care.

The Temple once again mobilized its high profile supporters to come to its aid, and Harvey Milk willingly complied. On December 20, 1977 – after he had been elected to the San Francisco board of Supervisors but before he took office – Milk wrote a letter on his campaign stationary to Joseph Califano, the Secretary of Health Education and Welfare (HEW). As he had before, Milk praised the work of Peoples Temple while the church was based in San Francisco.

> In this light, it seems outrageous that a group that has done so much for elderly, minority and disadvantaged citizens, is now deprived of its elderly members' right to receive benefits which have been earned through entire lifetimes' of hard work. Equally notable is that the Peoples Temple had been the first to defend the constitutional rights of others when they were threatened. But now it appears that their First Amendment right of religious freedom is being thrown into jeopardy. It is unthinkable that religious preference should preclude the fine and industrious members of Peoples Temple from receiving Social Security.

Among the documents recovered in Jonestown after November 1978 was the HEW response assuring Milk that all American citizens in Guyana, including members of Peoples Temple, were receiving their payments regularly. A scribbled note on the margins of the letter reads "Send to PT". Former Milk aide Daniel Nicolletta confirmed that the scribble is Milk's handwriting.

The Concerned Relatives received a big boost with the defection of top Temple financial assistant Debby Layton Blakey, on May 13, 1978. Leaving her mother, brother and husband in Jonestown, Blakey exacerbated her betrayal – in the Temple's eyes – by submitting an affidavit that provided ammunition in support of allegations made by Concerned Relatives. Blakey stated that Jonestown was nothing more than a concentration camp where people worked long hours under armed guard with little food. Five months after Blakey deserted the group, the Temple leadership was rocked with yet another top-level defection. Terri Buford, who worked with Blakey on the Temple's finances, left Guyana on October 27, 1978.

Armed with the Blakey affidavit, the Concerned Relatives asked California Representative Leo Ryan to investigate the conditions in Jonestown. A longtime friend of the congressman, Bob Houston Sr., also asked Ryan to investigate rumors that his son, a Peoples Temple member, was killed as he was preparing to leave the Temple. His son's two daughters had moved to Jonestown, and the senior Houston wanted to make sure they were not being held against their will. When Ryan read the Blakey affidavit, he began planning a trip to Guyana to visit, and judge, Jonestown for himself.

Responding both to the Concerned Relatives who were contacting members of Congress with their complaints about Peoples Temple, and to Grace Stoen's attempts to retrieve her child, the church asked its celebrity supporters, including Willie Brown, Angela Davis and Jane Fonda, to write President Jimmy Carter and ask him to intervene on the Temple's behalf. Again, Harvey Milk participated with a letter dated February 19, 1978, this time on official city letterhead. The letter is somewhat disturbing in that it reads as if it were written by a Temple publicist. Milk argues for Jones' paternity of John Victor Stoen. The supervisor refers to the unreliable declaration signed by Tim Stoen as irrefutable proof: "The most widely read columnist in the area, Herb Caen, printed Mr. Stoen's sworn testimony that John is not his child but rather Rev. Jones." Milk even goes so far as to ask Carter to take action against Tim Stoen, warning the whole situation could embarrass the State Department and jeopardize the international relationship with Guyana.

In reviewing this letter in more recent years, Milk aide Daniel Nicolletta expressed concern that it did not read as though it had come from his former boss and friend. Indeed, the letter to President Carter is very different from the rambling letter Milk wrote to the Prime Minister of Guyana almost six months earlier. The differences between the letters may be explained by a memo within the Jonestown files concerning a similar letter to Carter signed by State Assemblyman Willie Brown. The memo states that Brown would change the wording of the Temple's draft letter to the president. If the Temple ghostwrote both letters (and presumably others), and Milk accepted the language without making any changes, it would account for the different tones between the supervisor's letters to Carter and Burnham.

Cynthia Davis, Linda Mertle

Cynthia and Linda enjoyed life in the cramped quarters in the Geary Street headquarters, spending their time at church functions and meetings, while working on various Temple projects. Linda maintained a distant relationship with her father and stepmother, who were one of the few Temple families that kept their biological unit in tact. With the sole exception of Linda, the Mertles lived as a family, often taking in other Temple children, but always keeping their biological children with them. Contrary to Jeannie Mills' account in *Six Years with God*, in which she states that Linda chose to stay in the Temple as the rest of the family decided to leave, Linda recalls waking one day and realizing that every one of her family members was gone. They were no longer coming to meetings in San Francisco, and she could not find them when she went to services in Ukiah. People did not talk about defections, and for some time Linda thought that her family may have been called to go to Jonestown. But eventually the truth came out: they had left the church, changed their names, and abandoned Linda. They obviously did not trust their daughter enough to tell her about their plans to leave.

Because she remained in the church after her severe beating, Linda was able to command an attitude of toughness, eventually becoming one of Jones' favorite enforcers. She would be called on to beat other people, often larger and older than her, for a variety of infractions. As someone rose in the Temple, Linda thought that this type of behavior was the norm. It did not occur to her that she should refuse to participate in the beatings. After all, this was how her parents raised her. She looked around and saw adults, lawyers, nurses, all of whom willingly participated in these catharsis sessions. Even if she did not want to join in, she could not refuse for fear of another beating. But the discipline did not feel right to her. It was too much. The initial feelings of elation that came with winning her first boxing match soon gave way to the dull, muted, emotionless feelings of abuse. Instead of looking forward to the fights, Linda dreaded them, often wishing she could make it up to the person who was on the receiving end.

Linda shared her misgivings with Cynthia, who was having second thoughts about Temple life herself. Cynthia and Linda would sneak away and go for long walks talking about what life would be like for them on the outside. They fantasized about challenging the world together. Compounding their confusion about staying in the Temple was Linda's sincere desire to have nothing to do with moving to Guyana. She knew she was a city girl, and there was no way she was ever going to survive in the jungle. She did not even want to give it a try. They knew it was only a matter of time before they were called up to go to Guyana. Cynthia's brother, Emmett, had already gone down with his wife and newborn son, and her mother was constantly trying to convince her father to join the move.

While Linda wrestled with her options she was approached by Kay Henderson, who was also planning to leave the Temple. Kay, who was on the Temple's planning commission, told Linda about a plan by Temple leadership to whisk Linda away soon after her upcoming eighteenth birthday. Kay informed Linda that her parents were causing a lot of trouble for Jim Jones by holding press conferences and circulating negative fliers about the church. The Temple leadership felt it was best to have Linda in Jonestown, to use her politically to counter her parents' claims of abuse. However the Temple leadership also needed her parents' permission to fly the minor out of the country – something they would never get – so they had to wait until she became of age. This meant that Linda had a few weeks to figure out what to do before she was sent to Jonestown against her will.

When Linda told Cynthia about the plan to have her removed to Jonestown as soon as she turned eighteen, Cynthia agreed that they should leave the Temple immediately. About a week later, Cynthia started to get cold feet. She believed that Jones had paranormal powers and that they should tell him of their plans before he figured it out and punished them. Linda was horrified when Cynthia made it clear she was going to turn herself in; Linda decided that the moment had come to just leave. She called her mother, whom she had not talked to in years, and asked if she would be willing to come into San Francisco and pick her up.

But first she had a score to settle. She went down to the San Francisco Temple. She walked up to Penny Dupont, who had given her a hard time on numerous occasions, and literally punched her out. Afterwards Linda went to where she was to meet her mother. She never went back. She left everyone and everything she had known since her childhood, including Cynthia Davis.

True to her word, Cynthia confessed her and Linda's transgressions to the Temple leadership. Everyone at the meeting, including Cynthia, felt it would be best if she went to Jonestown immediately. She never returned.

$\mathcal{J}$ONESTOWN, $\mathcal{G}$UYANA

====================== 🞖 ======================

Vernon Gosney, Edith Cordell

$\mathcal{W}hen$ Peoples Temple relocated its headquarters from Ukiah to San Francisco, Vernon Gosney, his son Mark, and Mark's surrogate mother Edith Cordell joined the move. Edith and Mark settled into an apartment on Sutter Street, and Vernon moved into an apartment house on Potrero Hill where nineteen kids and six adults lived communally. The Potrero Hill commune was for troubled children, children with learning or behavioral problems, and those considered misfits or on the fringe even for the Temple. Edith took care of a number of Temple children, including children with severe physical disabilities, and Vernon got a Temple-sanctioned job in the law offices of Fred Furth.

During this time Lois Ponts took refuge at the Potrero Street commune. A nurse from Ukiah, Lois reportedly got in trouble at her job because she was caught stealing drugs for Jim Jones. Lois and Vernon soon began to conflict, leading to a confrontation in which Lois accused Vernon of molesting the children in his care. Vernon did not know if Lois was intentionally being malicious, or if she simply felt gay men should not be around children. Either way, it was a very anti-gay and hate-filled experience. Initially Temple leaders told Vernon to give up the children in his care until the issue was resolved, but Tobi Stone insisted that her son, Tracy, stay with Vernon. Tobi saw through the charges and refused to go along with the anti-gay witch-hunt. At a time when Vernon felt his credibility was on the line, and was not sure if he could convince people there was no truth to the charges, Tobi had come out unequivocally behind him. When Vernon moved to the Sutter Street commune with Mark and Edith, Tracy moved with him.

Many Peoples Temple members had already immigrated to Guyana, and Vernon, who had begun to experiment with drugs, decided the only way to stay clean was to join a thousand of his comrades in their jungle community. So, on March 19, 1978 – Vernon's 25th birthday – when Edith Cordell and the other members of their Sutter Street home left for Jonestown, Vernon and Mark went with them. While in Jonestown, Vernon worked as a laborer in the fields, and Edith assisted in taking care of both the elders and children of the community. She would also give haircuts to anyone who asked.

Secretly transporting over a thousand people from San Francisco to Guyana in a matter of months had been a monumental organizational task. When Temple members learned they were selected to go to Guyana, they got passports, quit jobs, and said good-bye to pets, friends and families. Oftentimes members would write to their relatives that they were going to their church's mission for a short trip, with no specific date of return. Those chosen to go to the Promised Land were moved into one of the twenty communal style homes, always had a small bag of personal items packed and ready to go, and waited for the call to go to Jonestown. Sometimes the wait was a matter of days, sometimes weeks.

When the date arrived for their departure, members of the leadership would show up to monitor the phone so people did not place any calls to non-members. The commune members were then driven to the Temple's building on Geary Street where final arrangements were made. In typical Temple organizational style, various tables were set up around the main dining room to facilitate the mass move, staffed with people to help with any legal or passport problems, to notify the Social Security Administration or people's employers, to handle medical and financial questions, and – at a "freak-out table" – to help people with last minute anxieties.

When all the paperwork was complete, the Temple members were often bused to other cities, and flown to South America via New York or Miami. Initially the Temple denied published reports it was abandoning its San Francisco headquarters, but it soon became obvious that Temple members were leaving the city for Guyana. Reporters found vacant apartments where once had been bustling Temple communes. The baseball team for Opportunity High School, an experimental high school for troubled and disadvantaged youth, lost thirteen players, all members of Peoples Temple, over the summer of 1977.

The Peoples Temple Agricultural Project, as Jonestown was formally known, carved out of the thick jungle of Guyana beginning in the fall of 1973. A handful of Temple members known as pioneers built housing, a central pavilion, schools, nursery, a laundry facility, and a radio room. They started a number of industries, and sustained themselves on native fruits and local fishing. After the main influx during 1977, hundreds of Temple members called Jonestown home, but the community never became fully self-sufficient, relying on shipments of supplies from its San Francisco headquarters. The small community needed everything to survive: hardware, house wares, machinery, laundry appliances, school supplies, clothes, food, supplements, medicines, and parts for repairs. Everything from nails to blankets was sent to the Guyana outpost from the Geary Street church.

Jonestown was created as an egalitarian community free of class, race or gender biases. Truly interracial communities, most of the members were either black or white, but there were also a handful of Latino, Asian and Native American people living in Jonestown. It anticipated becoming a self-sustaining community that would produce extra fruits and vegetables to sell or trade. Politically it was a challenging rejection of American society and more. Through their migration to Jonestown, a group of Americans had publicly disavowed the values that the U.S. government, at the height of the Cold War, was trying to impose on the rest of the world. According to Jonestown philosophy, capitalism and democracy were contradictory and could only clash; true democracy could be realized only through utopian socialism. Though Peoples Temple successfully created its own society in the jungle of Guyana, it was always with an eye to move to a more established socialist country, such as Cuba or the Soviet Union.

As Tobin Stone explained, The reasons Jones chose Guyana were many: "The main language, and the official one, was English; like his congregation, most of the population was black; the country was relatively close to home, making the transportation of people and goods less expensive than it would be to Africa. The new government – for Guyana had only achieved independence in 1966 – was socialist, though not strictly Marxist. Finally since the country was poor, it would be cheap to live in."

The Guyana government accredited the Jonestown School, and, in cases of emergencies, locals from the Amerindian population could seek out medical treatment in the Jonestown medical clinic. The community pumped its own water and used an electric generator for the lighting system at night. Temple members joined Guyanese political groups such as the Women's Revolutionary Social Movement, and marched in May Day parades.

Peoples Temple used its agricultural outpost as a public relations tool with the socialist government of Guyana in a number of ways. The Jonestown Express, the community's jazz and funk band, gave free concerts at political rallies in Georgetown. The Temple basketball team went to Georgetown in mid-November 1978 to play the Guyanese national team. The Temple had also scheduled a year-end event in Georgetown, which would have showcased its talents beyond the Jonestown Express, as well as its cottage industry products in a socialist display of songs, dance and political speeches.

A few weeks before the basketball tournament with the Guyana national team, Jim Jones offered some coaching advice, telling unidentified members of the team during a Jonestown meeting to show good sportsmanship by clapping when the other team scores and hugging their opponents in between periods:

> **Jones:** You can look stern on the floor, you can look sure of yourself, and be aggressive, but also be humble. And grab them between recesses and hug them before they leave. They won't know how to deal with it.
>
> **Male:** I don't know if they'll let you do it. I'll sure as hell try. I've tried before, and I've been treated like some kind of fag, like, I'm not going to the locker room with him.
>
> **Jones:** Well, shake hands. Shake hands with them.
>
> **Male:** I've always played that way. I believe in breaking down—
>
> **Jones:** Shake hands. I agree with you. I can see some idiot misinterpreting. Shake hands with them. If they don't want to shake hands that will make them look like assholes to all the people watching.

Jones does not correct the youth for using the term "fag," even though he would usually correct a person over the smallest of details. Even more telling is that he would categorize the person who thought a sportsmanlike hug was a reason to mistreat other players as an "idiot misinterpreting." In a small but interesting twist, a group that identified collectively as gay did not want to be perceived as a bunch of fags.

Gay relationships flourished in the community even though people were written up for unauthorized sex and public displays of gay-like flamboyance were discouraged in the Jonestown community. Vernon Gosney, who was scheduled to perform in the upcoming Temple variety show in Georgetown, witnessed this. Sharon Amos, the head of the Temple's Georgetown office, felt that Vernon was a bit too swishy to represent the community in the show. Vernon was told in no uncertain terms that he was not to be part of the pageant and was unceremoniously dumped from the performance.

Again we experience the dichotomy of a group that identified internally as being gay, but didn't want to be publicly perceived as being gay or – more importantly – as being weak. Gayness in men, whether in outward affection to other men or in overt homosexual appearance, was discouraged because of the perceptions of them as weak. On the other hand, strong women were portrayed as lesbians, and open lesbians were able to play important roles within the Temple's internal structure. Indeed, Jones is quoted as saying women should become Amazon warriors, going berserk at the sight of men. Overriding all other considerations, though, the Temple did not want to offend the sensibilities of others, specifically their Guyanese hosts. This is a classic example of traditional internalized homophobia, the "closet" mentality, where people tone down their gayness so they will not be mistreated, disliked or discriminated against.

The lush jungle environment inarguably offered a healthy alternative to life in the urban ghetto, but the surrounding jungle also served as a barrier from the outside world. Many Jonestown residents looked at their community as the last refuge against racism and rampant greed; they felt the jungle was protective. Others, overcome by the isolation of the community, had a different view of the jungle. To them it was as oppressive as any impenetrable wall, keeping them in and civilization out. Although most Jonestown residents experienced both sentiments at different times, Vernon Gosney hated the jungle community, and knew he had made a mistake the minute he set foot in Jonestown.

The arrival of new members complicated Jonestown's continuity, and conditions in the community worsened. The quickened pace of the exodus meant that there was little time to orient new arrivals before more fresh faces came. Despite the pace of the construction crew, the housing was insufficient to accommodate the new arrivals. Cottages that were initially built for four people, had bunk beds installed, doubling the occupancy, and then those people doubled up again. What was limited space for four people became confining quarters for sixteen. There was no privacy; oftentimes people changed their clothes outside in the open because there was too little room to move about in the cabins.

Daily life was regimented for no other reason than orderly organization. Meals were served in shifts, beginning with day laborers, followed by the able-bodied adults and seniors, and lastly the children; this would be repeated for both lunch and dinner. Laborers who were going to be too far away to return for lunch were given brown bag lunches. It was an intense organizational effort just to provide the daily needs of a community of 1000 people, not to mention the operation of a baby nursery, schools, a clinic, a sawmill and other industrial labors, fishing endeavors, and a working farm, as well as maintaining communication and supply shipments to and from San Francisco.

Monica Bagby

By 1977, Monica Bagby moved to San Francisco from Los Angeles to live with her mother Essie Clark and her two younger sisters. Essie Clark had been with the Temple for a few years and lived with her family on non-communal property owned by Peoples Temple. Monica enrolled at Opportunity High School along with a number of Temple youths, and earned her diploma. She had attended a few Temple services in Los Angeles, but once in San Francisco she attended regularly and volunteered to work in the communal kitchen at the Temple headquarters. Like other Temple members her age, Monica didn't join Peoples Temple because she wanted to, but rather because her family members already belonged to the Temple so her involvement in church functions was expected.

Essie Clark was concerned that Monica was running with the wrong crowd and becoming a negative influence on her younger sisters, so in an effort to save her daughter, Essie sent Monica to Jonestown on July 4th, 1978. At various times, Monica, like many members of Peoples Temple, both loved and hated living there. Jonestown confused her: she was attracted to the interracial community but repulsed and frightened by the level of violence that passed for discipline there. Additionally she felt too isolated in the remote South American jungle. Jonestown survivor Odell Rhodes remembered Monica, recalling that people in Jonestown listened mostly to rock and roll and gospel music until she showed up with her collection of jazz tapes, including Bob Adams, Al Jarreaux, Minnie Riperton, and Phoebe Snow.

Monica was not the only person in Jonestown concerned about the violence. By all accounts the discipline in Jonestown was tough. Those who defend the discipline in San Francisco argue that it was necessary because the Temple did not believe in calling the police to solve its internal problems. Following the migration to the remote jungles of Guyana, calling the police was simply not an option. As Vietnam vet Odell Rhodes recalled:

> There was discipline all right – no doubt about it. But, to me, it wasn't any big deal. You put a thousand people together and you damn well better have a little discipline. There's discipline in the army that's a hell of a lot worse – and then there's prison, which is a whole different ball game altogether. I don't doubt that things people say happened might be true, but the discipline I saw just seemed like the price you expect to pay for something like the Temple. I guess I figured if the Temple wasn't right for them, they shouldn't be with us. All I knew was that it was right for me.

When the Temple moved to Jonestown, the nature of the discipline evolved. Temple dissidents, those who asked too many questions or were too rebellious, were taken to the medical unit where they were sedated for whatever period of time was necessary. Additionally, the Temple would place troublesome people in the "box", a small confined area in a root cellar where people were essentially put in sensory depravation chambers for whatever period of time was necessary to make them docile. Physical violence in the form of mismatched boxing matches or beatings with a board were common. Usually a person being reprimanded was first put on the Learning Crew, a work crew segregated from the rest of the community that worked double time on heavy work projects. Children did not escape these discipline experiments either. An errant child would be taken to a well and lowered down to two waiting adults who would act the part of scary monsters.

Because the Temple attracted a number of violent criminals, it needed strict discipline to keep its rougher members in line. As the Temple grew and moved, it experimented with different types of discipline, often abandoning the more severe forms of punishment as counter productive. The Jonestown leadership said it disavowed the use of violence as discipline in Jonestown during the final months, but whether this was true or a public relations ploy remains unclear.

In addition to the discipline, Monica was concerned about Jim Jones' repeated calls for revolutionary suicide, a phrase coined by Black Panther leader Huey Newton. It was the belief that if people remained true to their principles, they would become revolutionaries, and that the state would react to the revolutionary vanguard with murder. Eventually, however, as Newton articulated it, the murders themselves would contribute to public understanding of the corruption of the state, and the revolution would succeed. Jones modified the philosophy: the secluded community was vulnerable to attack, and everyone in Jonestown should be ready to lay down their lives in its defense. Jones repeatedly talked about the unity of Jonestown and how individuals must surrender their identity for the protection of the whole. Monica, who did not want to be in the jungle, in the first place, was determined not to die there, no matter what the cause.

Loretta Cordell Coomer, Deanna Wilkinson

Loretta Cordell Coomer and Deanna Wilkinson remained a happy couple as they left the San Francisco Temple for Jonestown. Loretta had changed a bit since Harold left her, wearing less puritanical clothes and smiling more. She enjoyed her family, most of whom joined her in Guyana. In addition to spending her time coordinating the music for the Temple services, Loretta became the night supervisor in the nursery, while Deanna worked as a diesel mechanic in the Jonestown machine shop. Additionally, both women taught music classes in the Jonestown School. Deanna spent her free time rewriting religious and popular music to incorporate socialist themes and Jonestown references.

In a letter written to Jones, Loretta Cordell Coomer exhibits an acute awareness of racism and of the privilege that came with her white skin. She noticed the difficulty black women had in getting others to respect their authority. She confessed her attraction to strong black women and displayed feelings of solidarity and admiration for them. Loretta also felt the clothing distribution system in Jonestown was deficient. It seemed unfair to her that some people owned suitcases of clothes while others had only a few items. She felt it would be more in line with their communal and socialist politics to pool all of the clothing; everyone would have a few outfits and could turn dirty clothes in for clean ones. She believed her system would help eliminate any fashion-based elitism in the community.

At some point the fiery Deanna Wilkinson became concerned about developments in Jonestown. While on a trip to San Francisco she voiced her criticisms of the Jonestown leadership loud enough to be overheard. She was concerned the leadership was predominantly white while the laborers were black, and that people were not being fed enough. Deanna's concerns about the race-based power dynamics in Jonestown grew, and she began to show her discomfort by becoming more outspoken. Because of her stature in the community, Jim Jones had to be careful in dealing with her. He could not simply put her in the box or the medical unit to keep her quiet. Instead he summoned Deanna and gave her a very important assignment: She would join three prominent Temple members – Jones' wife Marceline, Temple financial secretary Terri Buford and Assistant Minister Jack Beam – in the Temple's attempt to lobby Congress in defense of Jonestown.

In March 1978, Deanna Wilkinson joined the Temple delegation on a trip from Jonestown to the nation's capital. The delegation spent a weekend visiting different members of Congress telling anyone who would listen about the good works of Jim Jones and Jonestown, and about the conspiracy by the members of the Concerned Relatives group to destroy Peoples Temple.

The decision was shrewd and disarming: Jones was able to finesse the temporary removal of an influential disgruntled member from Jonestown and put her to good use in the halls of Congress. She certainly could not complain about a lack of blacks in the leadership if she herself was representing the Temple. Deanna, however, was not willing to be bought off. A free trip to Washington, D.C., and more high-profile responsibilities for herself were not enough to keep her quiet. In May 1978, Deanna Wilkinson was assigned to the Learning Crew for an extended period because of her "immature, divisive attitude."

Tobi Stone

Tobi Stone, like Deanna Wilkinson, requested not to do any domestic work, opting instead for hard labor. She mostly chose to keep to herself in Jonestown. Her family was with her, including her children, and her shy, independent nature insulated her in the community. Tobi was a welder and wanted to learn how to operate the ham radio, Jonestown's only contact with the outside world. She was also an industrious and productive member of the construction crew, which was responsible for building the homes and various other structures in Jonestown. She loved her job, she wrote, and found fulfillment in "building these beautiful cottages the family lives in. I guess now I am just bringing out my talents here." Tobi took Swahili lessons from Pat Grunnett and after a short time changed her name to Tobi Chekevu Mtendaji, which means Happy Worker.

After a life-threatening asthma attack, Tobi wrote to Jones that she felt she should have died during the incident. She attributed her salvation to Jones and pledged her life to him. Like many members of the Jonestown community, Tobi felt that her life had been extended because of Jim Jones. Tobi went on to lament that American society was filled "with so much hate and deceit one becomes a militant in order to survive." She wrote about how she and her girlfriend in Jonestown, whom unfortunately she does not name, strived to live up to the principles of Peoples Temple, and how they welcomed the challenge. Although Tobi was a musician in Jonestown, she confessed she was easily embarrassed, but loved to be involved, "to be seen and not heard."

Cynthia Davis

Cynthia Davis quickly became acclimated to the difficult life in Jonestown. She enjoyed working on the cassava field crew, and on the Temple boat, going to various parts of the country to pick up supplies and bring them to the secluded community. Though she was not afraid of hard work, she found the pace challenging.

Cynthia was one of the many Jonestown residents interviewed by Dick Tropp, who was working on a book about Peoples Temple and the Jonestown community. Through this interview we are given insight to Cynthia's perceptions on relationships, lesbianism, and her on-going relationship with a man, and the power dynamics between men and women. Although Temple themes such as communism, abandoning relationships, and a challenge to sexist mores appear throughout her interview, it stills offers Cynthia's unique perspective as a religious African American lesbian on these issues. Her attraction to lesbianism was as much a rejection of men as it was an embracing of the gay culture. In fact she offers an insightful critical analysis of the role of lesbians in the feminist movements in America:

My becoming a lesbian was a very predictable thing. It came about as a result of the natural thing, the natural hurt thing that takes place when females interact with males. Women are brought up most of the time religious with customary male-female relationships. When you're eighteen, you get married and you live happily ever after. You raise a family and the whole trip. I'm not going to say I wasn't brought up like that. In fact that is the same ideas and hopes and dreams that I had. But when you get into relationships of course you get hurt and most times I felt that a relationship I got in, that's what happened – I got hurt. I got hurt so many different times so often ... People react to hurt from relationships differently. People react by going into dope scenes or they go into suicide or they go into prostitution. Some people are strong enough to learn to drop relationships altogether ... Some women, for instance, they go into a life of gays. They turn over for women. They develop a hate, like me, for example. I just developed a hate after so many hurts ... And this one particular time, it must have been the last hurt for me and I just decided 'skip it', skip relationships – period. I had thought about it. All girls wonder, all guys wonder about the life of gays and homosexuality and what it's all about. What is it all about? I guess I had the same thoughts about it ... I just tried it, you know. I enjoyed it. It was a new thing for me ...

To me it is quite obvious that you know yourself much better than you know someone else – meaning women know what women like. Women know what makes women unhappy and they know what makes them happy. You know what I am saying? So, it's like looking in the mirror. You treat a woman gentle because that's the way you would rather a man treat you. But you don't get that of course because men usually exploit women, their hopes and dreams. I mean they just – to me, men are – I don't know. Sometimes I think I don't understand them and sometimes I think I understand too much about them ...

There are issues in this male-female thing that do not break down easily. Why, for instance, if women are brighter and more sensitive, etc, aren't they more aggressive and acknowledged as leaders? To me, there is a reason for it. It's not the fact that women are as a whole scared or afraid to be in these positions or afraid to think those positions are afraid to take that stand in life. But I think it's … something that goes from generation to generation like witchcraft. It is the same thing with women in religion. It's a customary thing you do. Like women go way back as far as I'm concerned in oppression. It's always been said, "It's a man's world." It started out that way from Eve, and it's gotten better. But women haven't had the backing. They have the intelligence right? But the man has always had the stronghold on it. It's like having to be released from the chains. It's a holdback. The men have got the world and you just have to face it. They control the goods, they control everything that exists. It's up to women to beat the oppressor, or overcome the oppressor, in whatever move it takes. It's just something you have to accept. What you don't have to accept is keeping the chains – you don't have to accept that. You can work yourself out of it; women can work themselves out of it, if they pull together and bring themselves from under oppression …

For years I watched the women's movement in the states. I never believed in it; I always thought it was a bourgeois trip. I always thought it was a bunch of middle class women that got together in these little jive meetings to discuss bullshit. Taking off bras and beating up men. I always thought it was something they had to do besides having tea and cookies. They were bored so they got together and started talking about liberation, right? But I've never seen anything happen from it – all these unnecessary picket lines and these marches, newspaper interviews and television interviews and I've never seen it change anything. The only time I've ever seen any woman liberated was in this movement and the idea Jim Jones brought about. That's the only liberation I've ever seen in women period. That's the only time I've ever seen any oppression of women lifted … This movement is the only accomplishment I've seen of any kind. The oppression of women for instance, we've got that beat; homosexuality, gays – they do not have any trouble expressing themselves, there is no sexual persecution of them. You don't have any persecution of any kind of a background. Drug addicts, they're not persecuted, not here. Ex-cons, they're not persecuted here, not here. Gays, they're not persecuted. They're just people. We don't persecute racists; we don't persecute intellectuals. We don't persecute anybody. All we have here is people, working class, working together for the same ideas …

Teresa King, Diane Lundquist

Teresa King, who was fluent in Spanish, resumed her responsibilities of organizing a library, tutoring adults, and working in the Jonestown School. In an undated letter to Jones, Teresa expressed remorse about her relationship with Garry Lambrev. She felt that she had not been a strong enough friend to him and thus contributed to his leaving the church. Teresa confessed to Jones that she kept a number of Garry's poems long after she should have thrown them away, ultimately getting rid of the contraband when she was called to go to Jonestown.

Once they both moved to Jonestown, Teresa resumed her relationship with Diane Lundquist. In her capacity as Jonestown school supervisor, Diane worked with toddlers and preschoolers. Eventually the women had a falling out over Teresa's treatment of one of the children in her care. When Teresa was brought up on the floor, Diane publicly chastised her, only to have the community absolve Teresa of any wrongdoing after hearing her side. In her letter to Jones, Teresa reveals that she would rather go it alone than open up herself to be hurt by others. It is not clear if the women ever reconciled.

One of Teresa's responsibilities as Jonestown librarian was to coordinate the archiving of news reports and articles important to the community. Processing global news stories was one of the many techniques used by Peoples Temple to continually reinforce its political beliefs and worldview. Articles and movies promoting socialism, deriding capitalist society, and calling attention to the commonalities of oppressed people around the world were standard fare. Special attention was given to Soviet Union, Cuba, Angola, Chile and Iran. Occasionally the issue of homosexuality would come up in news articles about gay bashings or the religious right's attempts to further outlaw homosexuals. Coverage of California politics included the progress of the Briggs initiative, California's anti-gay teacher's bill, and Harvey Milk's electoral success.

Temple members wrote responses to Jones' sermons on the news to prove they were listening. Many of these written responses in Jonestown give insight as to how the community viewed the issue of homosexuality. More importantly, we see how the children of Jonestown were taught concepts of acceptance and compassion around the issue of gay men and lesbians unparalleled in American society at the time. Among the punishable offenses on the Jonestown playground was malicious teasing, which included making fun of someone else's sexual preference.

Loretta Stewart Cordell's teenage son Mark Cordell, who was raised in the Temple from birth, wrote in response to the Briggs initiative, "Gays are the best teachers, because they do not mess with children." Mark spoke from experience, because he was the very first boy known to have been molested by Peter Wotherspoon. This shows a clear understanding of the difference between pedophilia and homosexuality, often intentionally obscured in American society. Exhibiting a crucial understanding of the power dynamic between genders roles, Jeff Carey wrote, "I can see the need for males raised in capitalist society to face their homosexuality or more accurately to work on emphasizing their so-called feminine characteristics of sensitivity, to see their roles as oppressors and confronting their narcism [narcissism]."

Diane Lundquist adapted to life in Jonestown. She felt pride in building a truly communist community. She wrote home often, as did her sister Joan Pursley. Diane's mother Marilyn Pursley was so moved by her daughters' descriptions of the lush jungle environment she went down to the secluded community to see it for herself, bringing her third daughter with her. Cynthia Pursley was a very high-functioning person with Down Syndrome. Diane felt that Jonestown would be a better atmosphere for her sister than the cruelty she experienced back in the U.S. from the ignorance around anything and anyone who might be different from the norm. The leadership of Peoples Temple encouraged visits from sympathetic relatives to counter the mounting opposition from the Concerned Relatives group. Diane's mother welcomed the opportunity to bear witness to the growing community, and went down for a week's visit in early November 1978.

Congressman Leo Ryan was due to arrive in Jonestown on November 17th. Earlier that day, Marilyn wrapped up her trip, said goodbye to Diane and Cynthia, and had Joan accompany her to the airstrip. Filled with excitement about her trip to the secluded community, and confident that the congressman would be equally impressed, she had no idea that the politician, and all of the residents of Jonestown, including two of her beloved children, would be dead in a little more than twenty-four hours.

Several members of the Peoples Temple.

Terrence O'keith Wade

Diane Lundquist

Teresa Lynn King

Pat Grunnett

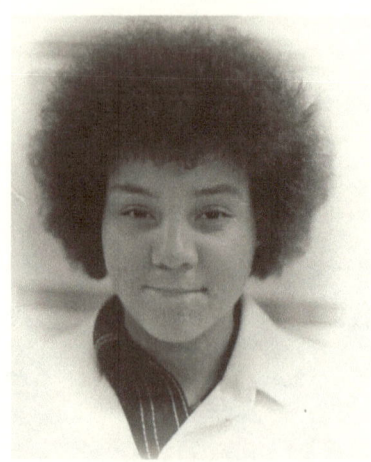

Deanna Wilkinson

Loretta Cordell

Edith Cordell

ＮOVEMBER *18, 1978*

＝＝＝＝＝＝ 🏶 ＝＝＝＝＝＝

Despite his best effort to adapt, and his sincere commitment to socialism, Vernon Gosney hated Jonestown. He simply wanted to leave. The place was so isolated, and there was no privacy at all. What surprised Vernon the most was how severely Jim Jones had declined. The dynamic healing preacher whom Vernon met that summer in Seattle in 1973 had become an apparent drug addict who rambled and slurred his words in paranoid rants about conditions in the United States. Jones would read the news over the community's sound system all hours of the day.

Vernon was injured while he worked on the citrus crew in the community's many orchards. He was taken to the clinic where he witnessed a number of Temple dissidents being sedated. Horrified, he watched Shanda James, Faerie Norwood, and Temple attorney Eugene Chaikin sedated and transformed into shells of their former personalities. He had a firsthand lesson on Jonestown discipline and realized that he would have to be cautious in planning his escape.

Expressing discontent in Jonestown was risky business though, and confiding in the wrong person often brought severe punishment. With no money and no passports, Temple members were told they would never survive in the hostile jungle. Even if they did make it to a local community like Port Kaituma, Temple leaders warned they would call the Guyana Defense Force and report a missing child molester, and that the member trying to escape would be arrested. Initially Vernon kept his desire to leave to himself. However, he eventually confided in his bunkmate and occasional lover Terrence "Keith" Wade, whose mother, Lue Ester Lewis, also lived in Jonestown. Like Vernon, Keith was a young, low-ranking Peoples Temple member who worked in the fields picking bananas.

Keith had arrived in Jonestown with his mom on December 3, 1977, and during his first week he was sent to work on the Learning Crew for having unauthorized sex with a man who was in an established heterosexual union at the time. In apologizing for his transgression, Keith stated that he would bring any future sexual interests up with the relationship committee, indicating that gay couplings were processed the same way as straight couples.

In addition to his time on the Learning Crew, Keith had been severely beaten for attempting to escape Jonestown. Keith and a friend, Jair Baker, pretended to be sick, so sick they would have to be sent to Georgetown. From there, they planned to go to the US embassy and fly to New York. However the Temple medical staff was too savvy to fall for two apparently healthy young men coming down with a mysterious illness and simultaneously requesting to be sent to Georgetown. After some serious questioning, the boys confessed, were brought up in front of the congregation, humiliated and punished. Because Keith had tried to leave the community before, Vernon hoped he could persuade the youth to join him in making plans to leave again. Instead of being a potential travel mate, however, Keith wanted no part of the conversation. Vernon accepted Keith's decision to stay with regret and respect, but continued with his plans to leave Jonestown.

After he recovered from his hospital stay, Vernon felt his best strategy would be to lie low during his time in Jonestown, not to make waves, or draw attention. Jonestown survivors Odell Rhodes and Hyacinth Thrash, both of whom wrote about their Jonestown experiences, agreed that it was easier to do what was expected of them than trying to buck the system in Jonestown. Index cards were used to record members' progress in the community. The ones for Vernon were all positive: he was credited for creative answers during classes on socialism and for volunteering to work extra hours.

Monica Bagby also volunteered to work evening shifts so she could skip out on the night meetings. Keith was a musician who was studying to be a nurse while working in the fields, harvesting bananas alongside Monica. Both being from Los Angeles, close in age and with similar tastes, they became immediate friends. Once Monica realized that Keith had tried to leave Jonestown, she approached him about her discomfort with the remote outpost, and her sincere desire to return to the United States. Keith harshly reprimanded her about being so open about wanting to go back. Such sentiments were considered the ultimate rejection of socialism and an embrace of a selfish and racist society. But he did not doubt her sincerity, and told her she should connect with Vernon. At least the two of them could commiserate together without fear of betrayal. It was not long before Vernon found he was face-to-face with a large black woman on a pathway that led to the Jonestown residents' living quarters. Staring into Vernon's eyes, she said, "Let's get the fuck out of this place."

Shock swept over Vernon. Was it a trap? Was she setting him up? For a second he was speechless. Vernon instantly decided to trust Monica but he was not sure why. That day they made a pact to do whatever it took, short of walking into the jungle, to leave Jonestown together. They were an unlikely couple: Vernon Gosney, a skinny 25-year-old white gay man, and Monica Bagby, an 18-year-old, heavy set, African American lesbian. Though they didn't know if, how, or when they would leave Jonestown, now they each had someone to share their forbidden desire to escape.

The first chance Vernon and Monica got to leave Jonestown came when longtime Temple member Lisa Layton died of cancer on November 8, 1978. As is customary when Americans die overseas, the American consul came to investigate the death and to issue a death certificate. As the consulate interviewed Lisa's son Larry Layton, Monica and Vernon found each other in the Jonestown crowd and worked their way to the man they thought was the U.S. official. However, they took too long to build up their nerve. As they decided to make their move – which would have called attention to themselves and exposed their desire to leave – the consul's group packed up and left Jonestown as quickly as it had come in. Initially upset at missing what they thought was their opportunity, Vernon and Monica realized the person they were going to turn themselves in to was in fact the consul's pilot. Had they notified the wrong person, they would have jeopardized any chance of escape. Indeed, other Temple members would have interceded, and they would have faced severe punishment. The close call did not deter them from their goal, though: they would try again to leave Jonestown.

About this same time, California Congressman Leo Ryan was preparing for his trip to Guyana. Extended negotiations between the congressman and Peoples Temple often devolved into a series of threats – Jonestown was private property well outside the authority of an American congressman – but arrangements were finally made for Leo Ryan to go to Jonestown in the middle of November.

The congressman was not viewed by the Jonestown leadership as an objective judge. Indeed Ryan had been writing letters to Temple members as early as May 1978, stating, "Please be advised that Tim Stoen does have my support in the effort to return his son from Guyana. In addition a long time friend of mine, Bob Houston, a wire service photographer, has told me his granddaughters are being held in Guyana." The residents of Jonestown believed that Jim Jones was the father of the boy, and that the boy had been abandoned by his "parents" when they left the church. They also resented Ryan's predetermined conclusion that people were being "held" in Jonestown. But Jim Jones knew that Ryan was coming and felt he faced a no-win situation. If he turned the congressional delegation away at the gates of the commune, it would only confirm the allegations of abuse and imprisonment. He was equally sure that if he let Ryan in, someone would want to leave the community.

Against this backdrop, Ryan, his aides, members of the Concerned Relatives group, and a number of reporters covering the trip, arrived in Jonestown on November 17, 1978. The residents of Jonestown were well prepared for the congressional delegation and provided a lively program of food, music and dancing for their guests. As the night's festivities went on, Vernon got close enough to NBC news correspondent Don Harris to pass a note that simply said: "Vernon Gosney and Monica Bagby, Please help us get out of Jonestown." It was another case of mistaken identity: he thought Harris was Congressman Ryan. Even more unfortunately, in his nervousness in passing the note, Vernon dropped it. The note did not go unnoticed, and from that point forward people in the Temple and Congressman Ryans' people knew Vernon Gosney wanted out of Jonestown. Both Monica and Vernon spent a sleepless night as they awaited the return of the congressional delegation.

The next morning Marceline Jones and a guard stopped by Vernon's job at the hospital to confirm that he did want to leave Jonestown. Thus she began a daylong attempt by Temple leadership to convince him to change his mind. When Vernon insisted he wanted to be interviewed by the congressional delegation, Marceline went to inquire about Monica. Top Temple lieutenant Carolyn Layton escorted him from his job at the clinic to the central pavilion and asked if there was anything the Temple could do to convince him to stay. He told Carolyn of his concerns about the Temple going to the Soviet Union because gay people were treated terribly there. Jim Jones had often preached about the mistreatment of homosexuals in both Cuba and the USSR. Carolyn acknowledged this, but argued that Vernon would always be part of Peoples Temple, even in Russia. But the dream of integration into the larger socialist community was an empty dream for gay or lesbian socialists. Instead of looking forward to going to the Soviet Union and fully participating in socialist society, many gays and lesbians were afraid for their lives. It was no comfort to Vernon that the people of Jonestown would settle in a country that was hostile to him. In a very strong way, then, his identity as gay was a contributing factor in leaving Jonestown. Unable to persuade him to reconsider, Carolyn left so Ryan aide Jackie Speier could interview him.

Initially Ryan and his aides were not sure how to interpret the reception by the residents of Jonestown. Indeed, all of the people they spoke to sang the praises of Jim Jones and Peoples Temple. However, Vernon and Monica's note was a clear indicator that some Peoples Temple members did not feel safe in saying publicly they wanted to leave Jonestown. Armed with this knowledge, when the congressional delegation returned to Jonestown on November 18, Ryan was determined not to be sidelined by time-consuming tours, and focused on defections. Soon eight members of the Parks family, who ran the commune's medical clinic, and six members of the Bogue family, who oversaw many of the agricultural aspects of Jonestown, also sent word to the congressman saying they had had enough and wanted to leave the community.

As the other Temple members realized people were defecting, the community fell into chaos. Many residents screamed and shouted at the defectors, while others simultaneously pleaded for community unity. Ryan was concerned about the safety of the people leaving the community. He accompanied Vernon to his cabin where he retrieved what few personal items he owned. As the men walked through the community, a number of people taunted and threatened Vernon. He was met at his cabin by a security team. They realized he was defecting, and asked him where he was going. In an act of defiance, he looked at them and said, "I am going back to San Francisco." Monica's luck was no better as Jackie Speier literally found herself caught between Monica and Temple security guards trying to block her from leaving her living quarters.

As Vernon watched the other families come forward and got processed at the pavilion, Ryan told him not to stray from the congressman's sight. This proved to be little protection. Jonestown security chief Jim McElvane approached Vernon from behind and lifted him off the ground by his neck, while taunting him, "Where you going, Vernon?" When McElvane less than gently returned Vernon to his bench, the congressional delegation finally realized what Vernon and the other people wanting to leave Jonestown were trying to tell them: there were no guarantees that anyone would leave Jonestown alive, and if they did, it was only because Jim Jones allowed them to go. The process for getting people to leave the jungle community noticeably hastened at this point with a new sense of alarm.

While waiting for Ryan to finish interviewing the other people wanting to leave, Marceline again approached Vernon. Marceline had always struck him as both efficient and motherly. Like many of the women who made up the Jonestown elite, she was nice, especially when she needed to be. As Carolyn Layton had before, Marceline asked if there was anything that could be said or done to convince him and Monica to stay. Marceline insisted their leaving was not necessary. She understood there were problems in Jonestown, but said the group was changing and adapting. She promised things would get better if they stuck together. At one point she asked him if he would stay were he permitted to be in an openly gay relationship. But staying was simply not an option for Vernon. He had waited too long to pass up this chance to leave, and feared the beating or sedation he most likely would receive if he remained.

When all pleas and arguments failed, Marceline asked that Edith Cordell bring Vernon's son Mark from the school area to his father at the pavilion. Marceline reminded Vernon that if he were to leave, he risked permanent separation from his son. But Vernon and Monica were without any resources and had no idea where they were going. He had not thought too far ahead of his escape. Lack of sleep, nutrition, and the constant blaring of the community's speaker system had left him confused and agonizing over his decision to leave. Despite his resolve, he still admired the community's goals and was not sure if leaving was the right thing to do. At the same time, he really did not believe Jones was going to allow the group to leave Jonestown alive. The only thing that was clear to Vernon was that Mark would be better off with Edith, his longtime caretaker. He could then make arrangements for Mark, and even Edith, to return to America when, or if, he got reestablished.

Like the other Jonestown residents, Vernon had signed custody of his son over to other members of the church right before leaving the U.S., thereby putting his legal authority over his own child in question. Marceline asked him to sign new papers giving custody of Mark to Edith. (He had previously signed custody to Debby Layton, whose defection six months earlier culminated in Ryan's presence there that day.) Complicating his decision to take his son from Jonestown was the fact that Mark had made real progress since he arrived. Mark's progress report from school showed that he was coming out of his shell since arriving, becoming more independent from Edith, and was making strides with the curriculum, including losing a speech impediment. Vernon's dislike for Jonestown did not change his belief that America was a racist country, hostile to his biracial son.

Temple member Phyllis Houston, who had arrived in Jonestown earlier that week ahead of the congressional party, told reporters she too planned to return to the United States, but like Vernon, she would be leaving her children in Jonestown, believing that the close-knit community was superior to life in America. Again we see the complex emotional games played by Jones: Peoples Temple spent a considerable amount of effort breaking down the natural bonds between people related to each other by blood, but if Jones felt a family member could be used to manipulate another, he did not hesitate to seize this opportunity.

Edith Cordell remained stoic. She had been a member of Jones' congregation since 1953 and had spent most of those 25 years as a close friend to the Parks and Bogue families. Her love for Vernon and Mark was as strong as the love she had for her own family. Years before, when Jones had gone to Brazil, Edith went to other churches with her family. Though she sent Jones money when he requested it, he was very upset when he came back to find that she had been worshiping regularly at another congregation. She soon began having premonitions that at the final hour, she would betray Jim Jones. Now she knew she was being tested. She could have simply walked over to Leo Ryan and told him that she wanted to leave too. Instead she held fast as she watched her relative Harold Cordell – who had begun a relationship with Edith Bogue after he divorced Loretta – and her close friends prepare to depart the community. Edith Cordell was determined not to let Jim Jones down again.

Jim Jones approached the various members who wanted to leave, trying to convince them to stay, and – alternatively – requesting that if they did leave, that they do so after the press left to save the community any public embarrassment. Vernon listened to Jones, but did not respond. Monica, on the other hand, felt she should let Jones know exactly why she was leaving. As Vernon recalls, "Monica Bagby was going to read Jim Jones' beads." She started angrily listing her complaints to Jones, until Vernon slyly stepped on her foot. He felt their chances of getting out alive were slim enough and did not think goading Jones was the most prudent path to take.

Eventually sixteen residents joined the congressional delegation and left Jonestown. In addition to the Bogue and Parks families, Vernon Gosney, Monica Bagby and longtime Temple member Larry Layton accepted Leo Ryan's offer to leave Jonestown. Vernon was alarmed that Larry had joined the group, as he felt Larry was too close to Jones and would never defect.

When the delegation arrived at the grassy airstrip at Port Kaituma five miles away from Jonestown, they were divided into two groups, and headed toward their respective airplanes. Monica and Vernon wanted to fly together, so they boarded the smaller plane with Dale Parks and Larry Layton.

As the planes were loading, the Temple's tractor and flat bed truck appeared at the far end of the airstrip, and the men on board opened fire on the congressional delegation. Simultaneously Larry pulled out a handgun and shot Vernon and Monica before Dale wrestled the gun from him. Killed in the attack were Congressman Leo Ryan, newsmen Don Harris, Bob Brown and Greg Robinson, and Temple member Patty Parks. Eleven others besides Vernon and Monica were seriously wounded. Monica was airlifted to Georgetown that night, and Vernon was flown out the following morning, both with life-threatening wounds.

Because of the important roles the Parks and Bogue families played in the overall function of Jonestown, their defections often overshadow those of Vernon and Monica. As Jonestown scholar Mary Maaga writes:

> Gosney and Bagby were average members without leadership
> positions. Their defections, although painful for those who knew

them well, and, perhaps, damaging because they indicated to the media that some displeasure existed among residents, would not have had any discernable impact on the management of Jonestown. Nor, seemingly, would the departure of Gosney and Bagby have contributed to the sense of despair and desire for liberation already present in the lives of the Jonestown leadership. The decision to leave by the Parks and the Bogue families, however, was a devastating blow for Jim and Marceline Jones and the leadership of Jonestown.

However, researchers to date have overlooked the threefold significance of the simple 11-word note passed from Vernon Gosney to Don Harris: it was the congressional delegation's first indication that people wanted to leave Jonestown; it tipped off the press to push Jones on tape about dissatisfaction among Jonestown residents; and it played an important role in triggering the Parks family's – and subsequently the Bogue family's – decisions to leave with Congressman Ryan.

Initially the contact between Ryan's party and Peoples Temple was upbeat and positive. All of the residents approached by the delegation assured the congressman they were happier in Jonestown than in America, and none of them wanted to leave. Of the more than 70 people interviewed at the request of the Concerned Relatives organization, none wanted to leave Jonestown. This really was no surprise, as people targeted by the Concerned Relatives group suddenly found themselves in positions of authority and leadership. By focusing on the very people they wanted to save, the Concerned Relatives elevated their importance to Jones and the Temple hierarchy, resulting in the exact opposite reaction hoped for by their relatives. Vernon Gosney and Monica Bagby were different. Without any support from family members on the outside – without family members in the Concerned Relatives – and with no support other than from each other on the inside, Vernon and Monica could make their plans to leave Jonestown, despite the odds or consequences, without being the focus of the unwanted attention.

That all changed with the eleven-word note. When Ryan confirmed that Vernon wanted to leave Jonestown, the congressman understood for the first time the magnitude of the situation. The note not only revealed the level of fear felt by some Jonestown residents, it also illuminated the very real chance for community-wide violence. Jackie Speier later recalled it was when they got the note that they first learned there was more to Jonestown than first appeared. Additionally Don Harris from NBC seemed to relish waving the defector's note in Jim Jones' face as he demanded to know how many more residents wanted to leave Jonestown. When the news media returned to

Jonestown on November 18, they had no intentions of going on a community-organized tour; they wanted to be close to Ryan in case more defectors came forward. All of this was of course in response to Vernon and Monica's note.

Lastly, and most importantly, the defections of Monica and Vernon may have had more of an impact on the decision of Dale Parks and his family to join Leo Ryan than previously realized. The Parks family was an important one in the Temple; many of them had been with Jones for more than two decades. When Jones heard that Edith Parks, the family matriarch, had also approached Don Harris about leaving Jonestown, he went to her and immediately began negotiating. At first, Jones was able to persuade the Parks family to stay in Jonestown until after the congressional delegation and the media left. However Dale Parks assessed the situation and came to the conclusion that if there was going to be any defections, and then the Parks family should join. Author Ethan Feinsod quotes Dale Parks as saying about Jones' offer to stay:

> They were the same kind of promises he had made to get me to come to Jonestown in the first place … I finally decided that the other people who stood up even before my family and said they wanted to go home would probably be enough to make him believe he was going to get a lot of bad publicity back in the States – and I knew he wouldn't stand for any bad publicity. I started to realize that if we stayed, we might well be involved in some kind of a murder-suicide situation, so I felt our chances were probably better if we went.

A small group of nine residents used Ryan's visit as an opportunity to escape by telling the Jonestown leadership they were avoiding the press and going on a family picnic. Initially, the Parks family intended to leave with this group, but waffled and changed their minds, deciding at the last minute not to join the small group of defectors. While that departure had gone unnoticed by the news media, Dale Parks feared the defections of Vernon and Monica were more public and would trigger the much talked about suicide, and convinced his family to leave with Ryan. Then, once it was clear that eight members of the Parks family were going, six members of the Bogue family immediately stepped forward.

Despite the fact they are often overlooked, if even mentioned by Jonestown researchers, Monica Bagby and Vernon Gosney, two of the many gay and lesbian Peoples Temple members living in Jonestown, were integral to the developments of November 18. This is not to lay blame on Vernon and Monica – indeed Dale Parks clearly feared that revolutionary suicide was inevitable in Jonestown – but in reviewing the series of events, their note should take its proper place in Jonestown chronology.

After the delegation left Jonestown, preparations were made to enact a mass suicide. There is much speculation as to why the community would choose to end its existence when the congressional visit had been a virtual success. But the fears of more visits and more defections, the impact of the defections of Debby Blakey, the Stoens, Terri Buford, and – that day – the Parks and Bogue families, as well as the earlier deaths in Jonestown of Lisa Layton and Jim Jones' mother, Lynetta, were insurmountable blows to the Temple leadership. Of course many will point to the ambush of Leo Ryan's group as the impetus for the suicide; still others will point to the congressman's visit itself.

Because Jim Jones had become addicted to a number of pharmaceutical drugs, his perspective on unfolding events was impaired. Survivors including Laura Johnston, who was in Georgetown on November 18, and Leslie Wilson, who was one of the nine "picnic" escapees, agree that Jonestown would have worked if Jim Jones had not been in the picture. Signs of stress were beginning to show as top level members defected and living conditions in the commune deteriorated. Many Jonestown residents watched their dream of egalitarian paradise devolve into a nightmare, referred to by Vernon "as nothing more or less than a socialist concentration camp."

Clearly the community was trapped, because Jim Jones was trapped. Jones was not able to return to America without facing a probing press, a number of civil lawsuits and possible criminal prosecutions. Blakey's affidavit outlined the conditions in the community from her perspective, and warned that the Temple leadership had held drills to prepare its members for mass suicide. Additionally the Jonestown leadership sent a letter to the entire United States Congress outlining their desire to live free of harassment and their commitment to destroy their community if not allowed to do so. Neither the United States government nor the Concerned Relatives took these repeated threats of self-extermination seriously.

Less than a month before their deaths, more than twenty residents recorded their feelings as the microphone was passed around a town hall meeting in Jonestown where they had apparently just voted to commit revolutionary suicide. The voices sound natural and unscripted but there are reoccurring themes indicating some degree of coordination. All of the voices are strong and adamant about their loyalty to the jungle outpost community and their desire to die rather than see it destroyed from the outside. The testimonies of Loretta Cordell Coomer, Deanna Wilkinson and Teresa King were caught on tape, and are provided here in their entirety. Their own words best answer the question of why these women would commit revolutionary suicide:

My name is Dianne Wilkinson. I am twenty-eight years old. And first of all I would like to let the world know that to live in America is a curse and especially if you're black. And the only place I have found that freedom and opportunity to become somebody in my life was in Peoples Temple. And meeting Jim Jones and his character and how he loved and took in animals and how he cared for each senior and child, yes we love our children, we love our seniors, but everybody here has made their own individual decision. I have made my decision that I don't want to live one minute. I would rather have my dignity than have to be on my knees begging for my freedom. And I would rather take my own life. Thank you.

My name is Loretta Coomer. At the age of forty I look back to back, 1953 and 54, when I was with Peoples Temple as a teenager. We moved from one church to the other because of harassment because of our stand for equality of races. Moved from one area of town because of cats being put down outside toilet, to another area of town where dynamite was put on our coal, to another area of town where glass was put in our pastor's food, to another city from there to another state, from there to another city, and then to another country where we are trying to find peace. Because of our stand for communism we have not been accepted anywhere it seems in the world and I feel that I am tired of running. And myself I prefer death tonight, being one of the last ones to speak I would like to be one of the first ones to die. Thank you.

My name is Teresa King and I also am voting for revolutionary suicide tonight. I was one of capitalism's casualties when I came here I was a drug addict and I was a drug addict because I didn't have anything to live for but since I have been here love has given me something to live for and I have seen this happen in the lives of everybody here. I also since I have been here I have been able to see that communism is what is necessary to bring this about. Before I came here I could only see what is wrong with society but I couldn't see what was necessary to bring about a change. The communal life that I have lived here has taught me that basically the problem is economic and the only way we will be able to change anything is through economics—

Teresa is interrupted by Jones who asked her: Why she chose revolutionary suicide over going to communist Cuba? She replies:

> Well I feel that in spite of the fact that communism is the answer, that we as a group are kind of premature in that what we have found here is more advanced than what other societies have to offer and I feel that if we went to another society that we would end up being another minority group and I feel that even the communist societies that exist have not dealt with racism to the extent that we have, or sexism and I don't think we would be able to live with it at this point after we have come as far as we have. Thank you.

Teresa's testimony alludes to the fact that gay men and lesbians had more freedom in Jonestown than they would in a socialist country. In response to another resident who also comments on Jonestown being more advanced then most socialist countries, Jones responds, "Maybe there isn't the level of tolerance that we would like to see towards those of different sexual orientation or the attitude that is so healthy here towards male and female [gender roles]." This indicates how concerned some members of the community were about moving to a place that was less accepting of gay people, and less sensitive to race and gender issues.

There is very little information about the last hours of the community. What is known comes from the recollections of a handful of survivors, and a 45 minute audio tape recording made during the estimated two hours it took for the community to die. After the congressman and his delegation left, the community gathered in the central pavilion as though it were one of its traditional town hall-styled meetings. Jones announced to the assembled congregation that the congressman's plane was going to be shot down, an event that would trigger a violent response from the United States military and the Guyanese Defense Force. Christine Miller, a Temple member from Los Angeles, asked Jones if the group could migrate to Russia, arguing passionately that too few people left for the rest of the community to give up their lives. Jones told the residents that the end was inevitable. The only question to consider was whether Jonestown was going to die on its own terms, or be destroyed by outside forces. During the whole process, the residents of Jonestown were led to believe they were coming to an independent conclusion, but it was an illusion of consensus, as the leadership had already determined the outcome. Despite Jones' request for dissenting opinions, the preparations for mass suicide were already underway. Syringes were prepared for the babies and young children, and different dosages were mixed for the children and adults.

How could the community presume it had the right to extinguish itself, an affront to the mores of most societies? The people who made up the Jonestown community may well have decided differently if they were given other options, but the end result facing them was death. The only question was how. One of the biggest obstacles to our understanding of the Jonestown tragedy is the reality that a group of adults could kill their children and seniors. Jonestown was disproportionately seniors and children, with able-bodied adults making up only a third of the population. Various members of the community discussed at length that they would rather have the children die by their own hands than be exposed to the violence, racism and poverty of America. One cannot rule out that many Jonestown residents may have thought that this was only a drill, and not realized that it was the real thing until people actually started to convulse and die.

Reconstructions make many people uncomfortable. However, it is safe to speculate Pat Grunnett comforted the children she loved so much, soon following them in death. Tobi Stone most likely rounded up her loving kids, and Edith Cordell probably clutched little Mark Gosney close to her as they died. Hopefully, Teresa King and Diane Lundquist were able to get beyond their differences before November 18, and maybe Diane was able to find her two children and Teresa among the Jonestown residents so they could die together. Loretta Cordell Coomer and Deanna Wilkinson, too, probably chose to die together. Soon after November 18, there was a rumor that Deanna Wilkinson had survived, but Temple member Laura Johnston and other Temple survivors knew Deanna would never have left Loretta's side. When Loretta was listed among the dead, they knew it was a matter of time before Deanna would be identified as well. As with all of the Jonestown residents who died on November 18, friends and relatives lovingly remember Keith Wade and Cynthia Davis.

Among the numerous writings left by the residents of Jonestown was an autobiographical outline for a book that Dick Tropp wrote and dedicated to Jim Jones. Though it is written while the Temple members were alive, it reads as a statement to explain how they felt towards America and towards each other in death. None of the many authors on Jonestown and Peoples Temple could have done a better job defining the people, politics, aspirations and goals of Jonestown than the residents of the community do themselves:

> We are America's offspring, many the children and grandchildren
> of a heritage of slavery and forced labor, painful realities quite
> the opposite of the ideals of freedom, justice, 'concern for the
> individual', that American society supposedly fosters.

> We, too, are the children, who searched the endless mean streets

of the rotted-out insides of decayed cities, unable to find the America we saw on television, and so we struck out in anger against the walls of our prison, the web of filthy streets held us in your nether-world.

We are the people who never fit into the slots. From whatever place we came, we had this in common: we sensed something was wrong, terribly wrong. There was a plague raging among us, a cancer eating away at America, and it had gotten into us, making us sick in a hundred ways. All the appearances of plenty, the supermarkets of consumer junk, the false symbols of affluence, the abundance that was really only one man's way of stealing from a million, only imperfectly covered up a terrible wound, a great festering ulcer that dug into the guts of our society, and our lives.

But it was often a subtle soul-sickness; with it came the dull weight of a feeling that nothing was of any use, that we weren't of any use ... even the old institutions of family and church that we took and sought refuge in were crumbling, and brought no relief, often just an intensification, a reminder of the pain, a reminder that we were nowhere, in a waste land of broken promises ... The slow death of knowing that someone could always take your place, that you really didn't matter, that you would be forgotten in a day as if you never existed ... For in that world anything could be taken away, and we never really had anything, anyway. The gradual death inside as our lives were usurped by machines, as we labored blindly to speed to the day of our own planned obsolescence, as we became mute, annoying statistics on someone's desk who we never saw, as we sought relief in a hundred addictions, as we became a welfare worker's case, a landlord's tenant, the boss's employee, an applicant, occupant, client, recipient, target audience, viewer ... while being told in the smiles of elegant advertising models and the puffy rhetoric of apologizing politicians that this was the best that the world had to offer in the way of a society.

From that slow death of the spirit, that nameless emptiness that penetrated through whatever we might manage to patch together to ward it off, many of us sought in desperation for a refuge.

We found each other. Our experience, our backgrounds were

what kept us apart, but our longing and sickness brought us together, in a realization that we are all victims. And it took one great honest human being who could remind us of that deeply-concealed truth, that ache of the spirit, and through his understanding, compassion and wisdom, his ability to penetrate to that depth and touch us at the heart of our heart's ache, out pent-up longings, deferred dreams, the answers to a thousand unanswered questions, and the endless, impossible contradictions of our lives – it took Jim Jones to bring us together, to heal the wounds by making us realize that we were hurting in common and hurting each other ... and that we needed to do something about it, that we were human, and all the same flesh and blood and mind and spirit, and needed each other, not the cheap props and cosmetics of advertising and politics, the celluloid and televised visions and excuses of what we could never be, not the sham-freedom of a society that was killing us!

We are the people of Jonestown ... we come from everywhere, from every corner of the nation, form every walk of life. And now, today, we have shaken the dust and filth of America's cities of despair from our tired feet. We ask what loyalty we owe our foster mother, America. We have drunk her bitter drink. We read her history books at her feet; we worshiped her gods, obeyed her rules, paid her tax-collectors to help fill her war coffers; ... we earned her pittance, only to have it ripped right back off in a hundred thousand ways, enticed, tricked, gamed, persuaded, tempted, suckered, cheated, and sold on junk and entertainment, fed on slow-acting, brain-curling fantasies, the shreds of fractured images and promises, the 'something' that only poorly shrouds the nothing, the great empty place of our lives into which all had disappeared.

The agony is that we tried to do something about it, but you wouldn't let us. You were determined to crush us with every weapon, and lie. Dozens of willing pawns have crawled all over each other for the chance to cast the first stones. Their target was a man, a leader of men, who worked right in the rotted-out center of your cities bringing people security, a true family that would be like a shelter, a protective wall and a source of strength to the people. And many came to the house of Jones. From every segment of society ... People whose lives were like the caged animal who gnaws at himself, then nurses his own wounds, and only half-aware of why, confused by the pain. They came to the house of Jones, casting away old idols and superstitions, bad habits and wrong decisions, prepared to be remade, into regenerated human beings, molded into a unified family, our best potentials and capacities for service and responsibility brought out and nurtured in the sunlight of Socialist cooperation, under a resolute and fearless leader/father/teacher who is devoted to his ideals and cannot ever be bought off, compromised, deterred, or fooled.

We finally found someone – or did he find us? – who could give a voice and eloquence to that outrage, who spoke for us whose tongues were broken, who could pull the weeds from our confusions, and direct our eyes and minds past uncertain images, the misunderstood motives, the longings, the not-knowing-why, the deferred dreams … He woke us up out of the sleep of the oppressed. He showed us where we were, who we were, why we were, what we were … Now, having seen the handwriting on the wall, having seen that his work would never really succeed as he wanted to, in an environment that was inhospitable and increasingly hostile, he began this community.

To our foster mother America, we say: we are an attempt to rediscover you, the "America" that never lived up to its promise and ideals of liberty and justice for all, and have finally given up. We didn't do this because we wanted to – it was necessary. Now we have a change … We are not anti-American; we have always been the best friend America ever had, and still are. We are your profound critics, your very own children. And under Jim Jones we have tried to develop for many years solutions to the crises in our land. But we were not about to let our leader and our movement become another in the graveyard of civil rights and progressive groups that have been back-stabbed, sold out, or who have subtly abandoned their aims and vision, lulled and tricked by the shapes, symbols, rhetoric and empty promises of the real traitors against the American people. Or who have been decimated by troublemakers and provocateurs from within or without.

So we have come here, the people of Jonestown, and we have come to build. We have our remorse, our bitterness, and our scars. They will never go away. But Jim Jones has always believed in lighting candles rather than cursing the darkness. And we are determined here to let our light shine ... We will reclaim freedom's birthright. We will discover America in spite of you."

Harvey Milk And Peoples Temple

================ ⌗ ================

On November 27, 1978, Dan White, a former San Francisco City Supervisor, entered City Hall through a basement window, went to the mayor's office and killed Mayor George Moscone. He then proceeded to the supervisors' chambers where he shot and killed Supervisor Harvey Milk. San Franciscans were still reeling from the news that was coming out of Guyana. Reports – and hopes – that hundreds of Jonestown residents tried to save themselves by running into the jungle turned out to be unfounded, as the total number of dead continued to climb, eventually surpassing the nine hundred mark.

Because of the proximity to the Jonestown tragedy, and the political connections between the two slain political figures and Jim Jones, there was immediate speculation that the rumor of a Temple hit squad, called "the Angels," was involved in the City Hall murders. However, Dan White soon turned himself in to the police. After resigning from the Board of Supervisors, White had changed his mind and requested a reappointment. Milk had successfully lobbied Moscone to turn down the request. The subsequent murders were a result of rage.

Milk's murder elevated him to the status of martyr for the gay community, which immediately began sanitizing Milk's image. In the wake of Jonestown, that meant obscuring his relationship with Peoples Temple. Rumors immediately surfaced that Milk was angry at the Temple for using his name on their promotional material after the bad press of the *New West* article appeared, over a year before his murder. Another report claimed that Milk was closely monitoring the Leo Ryan trip and was going to reevaluate his support for the Temple if Ryan's trip had validated any of claims of abuse or malnutrition. Though Milk may very well have distanced himself from Peoples Temple after the Ryan visit, he gave no indication he was ever considering such a move. Milk made no public comments in the aftermath of the Ryan murder and the Jonestown tragedy that he had any intentions of renouncing his loyalty and support for Peoples Temple.

The other rumors also turned out to be without foundation. Milk's letters uncovered at the California Historical Society refuted the claim that Harvey Milk was dismayed by the Temple's use of his name in promotional fliers. To the contrary, the letters indicate an open and mutually supportive relationship between Milk and the Temple right up until mid-1978, and the Temple continued to use Milk's name in its promotional material from 1977 through 1978. Along with City Supervisor Carol Ruth Silver and 75 other prominent San Franciscans, Milk was listed as a Temple supporter and endorser of the Temple Benefit and Support Dinner, which was to have been held in December 1978. California State Assemblyman Willie Brown was to have been the master of ceremonies. Milk had ample time and opportunity to publicize his concerns about the Temple's use of his name if he had any. These concerns would have be recorded somewhere, and certainly would have been recalled by Milk staffer Dan Nicolletta.

Milk explained his loyalty in a *New York Times* article announcing the cancellation of the support dinner. "A year had passed and the Temple had been investigated by the district attorney, and no one was taking them to court." He saw no reason to withdraw his support. If the allegations against the Temple could not be substantiated – which they had not been so far – then the Temple was innocent. The Temple had been tried in the press and not in the courts, Milk said.

Milk actually seemed to go out of his way to make sure the Temple was involved in his politics. When friends of Milk hosted a coffee reception for Chip Carter, son of then-presidential candidate Jimmy Carter, Milk made sure Temple members were invited and given an opportunity to talk to the influential young man. Additionally, after Milk arranged for Temple members to perform at the Castro Street Fair, he invited them to attend the post-fair party. Despite bans on drinking and associating with non-members, representatives from Peoples Temple attended these events and others like them.

Evidence of Milk's loyalty to the Temple after the *New West* article is best illustrated by Milk himself, not only in his letter to the *New West* editors but also in a column he wrote for the gay newspaper *The Bay Area Reporter*. Milk titled his column "The Milk Forum" (it is not clear if he borrowed the name from *Peoples Forum*, the Temple's newspaper.) The column responds to attacks on the black community in America in general, and on the Temple specifically, and charges that the bias that fuels these attacks is the same bias which fuels attacks on gays and lesbians:

> We must reach out to every group – be they political, environmentalist, labor or minorities. We must not allow the reactionary forces to continue to divide us … The most powerful church in this city that spoke out over and over for Gay rights is a church that is mostly black. It is one that has started to use itself politically. The Catholic Church – which uses itself politically – is okay to the media. But a black church that strongly fights for Gay rights is now being attacked for being political! I'm surprised that the reactionary forces took so long to attack the Peoples Temple. Democracy is a strange thing. Religion is a strange thing. And both are misused in this nation … We had better find our 'social' friends and join together before the reactionaries turn social issues into political issues. Freedom is not a political or an economic issue. It is a right. And that right is under attack.

Sentiment reinforcing Harvey Milk's support of the Peoples Temple also comes from a letter from Jim Rivaldo, a close friend of Milk, who wrote to Jim Jones on July 28, 1977.

> I felt honored and privileged to be a guest along with … Harvey at your services last Sunday. I have long admired the Peoples Temple and Rev. Jim Jones for your courageous stands in support of human and civil rights whenever and wherever these rights have come under attack … I trust as Peoples Temple and Rev. Jones come under increasingly close scrutiny, you will win vindication and emerge even stronger and more committed to the ideals you expressed so eloquently and to which the congregation responded so movingly. I try my best to live up to those same ideals in my own life and although I haven't had much direct contact with Peoples Temple I have derived strength from your example.

Further evidence of Milk's continued support can be found in an internal Temple report from four members who attended a fundraiser for U.S. Congressman John Burton. A short note at the bottom of a memo written on October 15, 1977 reads: "We saw Harvey Milk who was the same Harvey – friendly, telling us the press coverage had to improve and the tide had to improve sometime." Had Milk avoided the Temple delegation or questioned them about the Temple's use of his name in their literature, these members would have reported it back to Temple officials via this memo. Indeed that is the very purpose of the memo. Clearly, Harvey Milk and his close circle of friends supported Peoples Temple well after allegations of Temple-inspired break-ins and other crimes hit the newsstands.

Stories circulated of a falling out between Harvey Milk and Jim Jones, earning Milk a place on Jones' hit list of political enemies, but there are no reliable references supporting this claim. It should be noted that a number of people who did not want to be quoted by name stated that the general perception in the gay community at the time was that there was a falling out of some kind, and Milk insiders, including top aide Anne Kronenberg, initially felt that his murder was somehow a result of his relationship with the Temple. However, the number and tone of the letters from Milk, either to Jones or on behalf of the Temple, indicate an amicable relationship between Jones and Milk in February – possibly as late as June – of 1978. Additionally, the letters that Temple members sent to Milk after the death of his lover Jack Lira in September of 1978 indicate Milk was certainly in Jim Jones' good graces at that time. There does not seem to be enough time or, more importantly, any apparent reason for the Milk-Jones relationship to deteriorate so drastically in the two months between the receipt of the sympathy cards and the tragedy on November 18. One must conclude the rumor of a falling out between Milk and Jones was a mechanism used by Milk's supporters to distance Milk from Peoples Temple in light of the universal condemnation, alienation and ostracism experienced by its surviving members and supporters after the Jonestown tragedy.

An example of this can be seen in the description of the sympathy letters sent in October 1978, from Jonestown to Milk that appeared in Milk's biography, *The Mayor of Castro Street*: "Even then [before the Jonestown tragedy] the packet of letters was chilling. It was as if it had never crossed the writer's minds that the appearance of exactly fifty letters – many of them identical word for word, and none of them wavering from condolence-invitation formula – written on identical pieces of paper with similar pencils would look like anything but a spontaneous outpouring of sympathy."

Contrary to this depiction, there were over fifty letters sent to Milk, and none of them were word for word. Though they do stick to the condolence-invitation formula, they are all on different stationary and none of them are written with pencil; indeed some are even typed. Although it was probably clear to Milk that the letters were not spontaneous (anyone who worked with the Temple knew that Jim Jones called the shots), it can not be ignored that they were, nonetheless, a statement of support and solidarity from the residents of Jonestown. It is not clear why a respected reporter and author like Randy Shilts would take such liberties with the truth (or how much leeway he took with the rest of Milk's biography), but by focusing on the number and description of the letters, he deflects their overall significance: they are reflective of a close relationship between Milk and Jones.

To highlight the need for caution, Nathan Landau writes in his book, *Heavenly Deceptor*:

> John Crewdson, a reporter studying both the Jonestown deaths and the Milk/Moscone murders notes that like Mayor Moscone and a number of other prominent California politicians, Mr. Milk had publicly endorsed the Peoples Temples and Jim Jones. Milk had spoken often at the Temple and had even been invited to visit Jonestown as an honored guest; he declined. Crewdson quotes Milk as saying that Guyana was a great experiment that didn't work.

Landau's work was used as the basis of a January 1999 article in *USA Today* which reads in part: "[Milk] saw Guyana as an experiment that didn't work. Milk disassociated himself from the Temple and believed that Jonestown political forces were plotting his death to silence him. He was right." Closer inspection of the original article cited reveals there is no disassociation on Milk's part, and Milk's assessment that Jonestown was a failure may not have been so concrete. Crewdson's original article reads:

> Like Mayor Moscone and a number of other prominent California politicians, Mr. Milk had, until the time of the murders and suicides in Guyana last weekend, publicly endorsed the Peoples Temple and its founder, the Rev. Jim Jones.
>
> In an interview a few days before his death, Mr. Milk said he had spoken at the Temple once or twice, principally because early on it had supported the homosexual rights movement. He said he had been invited to visit Jonestown, the cult's settlement in Guyana, by Mr. Jones but had declined.
>
> 'Some day this will make a great opera and I'd sure like the rights to it,' he said. 'Guyana was a great experiment that didn't work. I don't know, maybe it did.'

Milk does refer to Jonestown as "a great experiment," but the conclusion that he felt it was a failure is less clear. That Milk would even slip in this comment at a time of ostracism and vitriol spewed at the surviving members of Peoples Temple and their supporters' gives hint that he was open to other interpretations of the end of Jonestown than the one that gained currency in the immediate aftermath. To even half-heartedly propose that there may have been more to Jonestown than failure, indeed that on any level it may have worked, was a rare reaction. Most politicians whom Jim Jones supported – including Willie Brown, Joe Freitas, Richard Hongisto, and Art Agnos – could not distance themselves from Peoples Temple fast enough, but Harvey Milk proposed to *The New York Times* that Jonestown might not have failed. Other than the article about the Temple support dinner, this quote is the only known, recorded direct reference Harvey Milk made about Jonestown. (However, Laurie Efrein Kahalas, the press person for the San Francisco office of Peoples Temple at the time, recalls a phone call from Milk soon after the November 18 tragedy. He expressed his condolences and support for the surviving members.)

The Randy Shilts' interviews of Milk's friends conducted about four years after the November tragedies indicate that Milk was "shocked" by the deaths in Guyana. A number of people recalled that Milk began telling a series of off-colored jokes concerning the Jonestown suicides, namely that the suicides themselves would have made a great opera. This was classic Harvey Milk, formerly a professional clown, who told tasteless jokes as a way to cope after his lover committed suicide. Shilts initially tried to use the jokes to distance Milk from the Temple. His editor crossed the jokes out, however, with an admonishment in the pages' margins that the use of the jokes was too harsh, and an unflattering reflection on Milk.

Milk's friend Tory Hartman told Shilts that after November 18, the San Francisco Police warned the supervisor to move into the back rooms of his apartment, as a precaution. Whether they contacted him on their own or were responding to his concerns is not clear. Hartman also recalled running into Milk at Cliff's Variety Store soon after the Jonestown suicides, and he confided to her he had made a tape. The contents of this tape have yet to be uncovered, and Hartman can no longer be located.

Why Milk might believe members of Peoples Temple would want to put his life in danger is not made clear from the interviews. Milk could have very well feared the Temple because of his previous pledges of loyalty to Jim Jones. Certainly Milk must have been haunted by his notes: "If you take one of us you must take all of us, sign me up," as well as "my name is written in stone in support of you and your people." These clearly could have been the source of Milk's concern.

It is also worth noting that the FBI seemed specifically interested in the rumor of Temple hit squads and asked a number of the Temple defectors if they had any knowledge of who was on the hit list. The FBI repeatedly and pointedly asked about any connections between Milk, Moscone and the Temple. All of the defectors were asked about the "Angels." The survivors offered little or no information as to who was on a political hit list, or more importantly, why.

This evidence undermines the rumors that Jim Jones recruited Dan White to kill his political enemies, beginning with Harvey Milk and George Moscone. The correspondence uncovered to date seems to indicate the opposite would be true. Moreover, while in San Francisco, the Temple had incurred the wrath of a number of politicians, including then - City Supervisor Quentin Kopp, Kopp had been thwarted in his attempts to investigate Peoples Temple and its influence in the 1976 elections. After the deaths in Jonestown, he demanded an investigation into whether the Jonestown tragedy, and the murder of U.S. Congressman Leo Ryan, could have been averted if his earlier calls for investigations were heeded. Clearly, if Peoples Temple had political enemies on the city's Board of Supervisors, Kopp's name would have come up long before Milk's.

Additional support for this belief is the revelation that Dan White had also planned to kill City Supervisor Carol Ruth Silver and California State Assemblyman Willie Brown. Silver was one of only three city supervisors to endorse the Temple's support dinner, and Willie Brown was one of Peoples Temple's most prominent political supporters.

No theories, much less hard evidence, have been put forward as to why Jim Jones or members of the Temple's hierarchy would want to assassinate its top four political allies. Rather it is more logical that Milk, Moscone, Silver and Brown would have been targeted by Temple opponents for the exact opposite reason: they were political supporters of Peoples Temple who may have demanded independent investigations into the tragedy of Jonestown, and the murder of Representative Leo Ryan.

The final rumor concerning Harvey Milk and Peoples Temple is the persistent story that he asked to have grape Kool-Aid packets be scattered with his ashes. (Kool-Aid was erroneously reported as used in the final Jonestown concoction; in fact Jonestown leadership opted for Flavor Aid.) Randy Shilts mentions that Kool-Aid packets were scattered in the bay with Milk's ashes, but he gives no indication of what it meant. Interviews conducted for this book revealed that Milk's friends added the grape Kool-Aid in a light-hearted attempt at making fun at the relationship between Milk and the Temple. Nothing more can be read into it because, according to Milk insider Daniel Nicolletta, Milk had no prior knowledge of the act, contrary to persistent speculation and rumor.

It is not clear if this is the complete collection of all correspondence between Milk and the Temple. Indeed, other letters may eventually surface. For example, Jones aide Sharon Amos states in her personal notes that while she was meeting with a Guyana Minister of Parliament, Carrie Ramsaroop, on June 4, 1978 she delivered a letter of support from Harvey Milk. It is not clear to which letter she is referring, but it is either the one written to President

Carter in February, or one yet to be uncovered. It seems unlikely that it would be a copy of the letter sent to the Prime Minister of Guyana, because Milk wrote that letter before he was a supervisor. Presumably the Temple would present Ramsaroop with a current letter on San Francisco City letterhead, but not necessarily. Also, one of the tapes which the FBI recovered in Jonestown apparently included a speech given by Harvey Milk to the Peoples Temple congregation at one of his many speaking trips to the church. The FBI's index of the contents of Peoples Temple tapes recovered at Jonestown is incomplete at best, and the tape has not yet been located among those released to the Jonestown Institute, which oversees the transcription of Peoples Temple tapes. Eventually, though, we may hear Milk's own words to Peoples Temple.

The evidence uncovered in recent research presents an alternative to the unflattering image of a vote-greedy Milk using the likes of Jim Jones to get elected but cleverly maintaining a distant relationship from Jones. Instead we have Milk, who stood by his political allies, just as they stood by him in the fights which were important to Milk, specifically the Bryant and Briggs initiatives. Though Milk may have warned his aides to be on their guard around Peoples Temple, we know from his own words of the support and admiration he had for the works of the Temple. One would have to believe Milk to be quite cynical to claim the letters sent to Jones were just political expedience. In their attempts to separate Milk from Jim Jones and Peoples Temple, historians and biographers have overlooked, downplayed or flatly distorted the truth. Hopefully we will now begin to understand why Milk supported Peoples Temple, and why we might want to reevaluate our criticisms of it. It is important for those who value preserving Milk's memory that we do not engage in sanitizing the facts, or in letting the biases against Jim Jones and Jonestown be an excuse to cover up or even change history.

$\mathscr{C}$ONCLUSION

Since November 18, 1978, people have tried to place responsibility for the deaths in Jonestown on someone, anyone. Many of the defectors feel the blame falls squarely on the shoulders of Jim Jones. Others think every adult in Jonestown shares some responsibility. Some people blame the Concerned Relatives group for the pressure it put on the Temple leadership, as well as its disregard for the threat of the Jonestown community to extinguish itself, as definitive factors. Some Temple loyalists include the federal government's intrusion into their community, and a few single out the CIA. Even gays were tarred with the same brush. As Forbes Burnham, Prime Minister of Guyana, stated, "Homosexuality and suicide are the symptoms of a rich society." Although Burnham had been considered one of Jones' closest allies, his post-tragedy analysis seems to link homosexual sex and death.

But the responsibility lies, again, somewhere in the middle. Though Jim Jones was able to manipulate many, he would not have had such success if America was more compassionate toward its poor or marginalized citizens. Indeed, as the Black Panther Statement on the Jonestown Massacre states:

> The Black Panther Party charges the United States government, specifically the Central Intelligence Agency and the U.S. Department of Defense, with the murders of over 900 innocent men, women and children at the Peoples Temple settlement in Jonestown.

> The Party demands an immediate citizens' investigation into the Jonestown tragedy. In no way should this investigation be organized or controlled by the American government, which *alone* bears the responsibility for viciously slaughtering a group of Black and poor people who left the oppression of this country to build a society where there would be none.

We must not be tricked by the CIA-created mass hysteria and confusion that is sweeping through the country about the Jonestown massacre. If there were freedom and justice for all in America, there would have been no need for Jonestown in the first place. If Black and poor people could live in peace and dignity in this country, those 900 people who told the world they found perfect happiness in Jonestown and, under no circumstances, would give it up, would not be in their graves today.

The true responsibility for Jonestown will most likely be debated well into the future, but all indications are that the government was monitoring the activities of Peoples Temple on a number of levels. The history of the government's infiltrating and monitoring leftist groups during the late sixties and seventies, the political nature of Peoples Temple, and the international implications of the Jonestown settlement, all give credence to reports of government's monitoring of the Jonestown community, especially in light to the numerous complaints to the Postal Service, Social Security Administration, the Federal Communications Commission and U.S. Customs. The CIA clearly had operatives on the ground in the form of Richard Dwyer within the US embassy, and was the first agency to report back to Washington in the early hours of November 19 about the deaths in Jonestown. There will never be certainty of the government's role in the final days of Jonestown or the full burden of responsibility it should bear until these agencies open all their records to historians and researchers.

However, we can explore the many reasons Jim Jones was so popular, why nearly a thousand members of Peoples Temple would leave America to build a new home. Who were these people, and why did they make the series of decisions that led to the events of November 18, 1978? The experiences of gay and lesbian Temple members may not have differed all that greatly from those of their heterosexual counterparts, but it is important to explore these issues to see if gay people are more inclined to join groups, and if so, whether they occupy positions of power, whether they are respected by other members in the group, and if their gayness impacts their decision making process.

A census taken in Jonestown on August 30, 1978, reveals there were no more than 73 "officially married" couples at the commune. This accounts for 146 people in a group of over a thousand. Taking into account the children in the community, as well as residents who disavowed sex altogether, there must still have been a substantial gay and lesbian population, including a number of avowed lesbians on the "marriage list."

In Jonestown, gay and lesbian people were given positions of authority: Deanna Wilkinson, Tobi Stone, Keith Wade and Diane Lundquist were all cottage supervisors, and Loretta Cordell Coomer, Pat Grunnett, Teresa King, and Deanna were members of an elite group that was approved to speak with dignitaries and other visitors to the compound. As Temple member Laurie Efrein Kahalas wrote,

> There was complete acceptance of gay people in Peoples Temple – there was even more acceptance of gay relationships than of straight relationships. I think part of that from Jim Jones' perspective was that gay people could be more counted on to relate to persecution, but that straight couples were more likely to be narcissistically self-involved and shut others out ... I think gay people felt more secure ... As an advocate for gay rights, Jim Jones was 100%.

An important factor to keep in mind while researching information on Peoples Temple, from a gay perspective, is how mainstream writers treat the relationships in Jones' inner circle. The women who comprised the inner circle of the Temple are often referred to as Jim Jones' mistresses, and indeed many of them were. But the relationships between Jones and the male members of the inner circle are viewed as far less intimate. When Jones is referred to as having sex with a male member, it is to degrade or humiliate him. For example, Jim Jones and Grace Stoen are described as lovers; however Jones' relationship with Grace's husband Tim Stoen, whom Jones looked to as a brother and partner in developing the church, is not portrayed the same way, despite evidence of a long relationship. Is it so hard to believe the three of them, at one point, loved each other equally? That the love between Jim Jones and Tim Stoen was just as strong if not stronger than the love either of them had for Grace? As author Ethan Feinsod puts it, "as far as Grace could tell, if Tim was married to anybody, it was to Jim Jones. In terms of time spent together, emotional closeness and shared experience, Tim and Jones were far closer to each other than either was to Grace." When we remove the monogamous hetero-centrist view, we see a group of people where men and women interchanged partners, loving many of them equally, in a true communal experience. Also, no substantive attention has been given to the potential existence of lesbianism or bisexuality between the women in Jones' inner circle, and there is very little information to build reliable conclusions.

Some will argue the Temple failed its gay and lesbian members. But in light of the roles Deanna Wilkinson, Loretta Stewart Cordell Coomer and Pat Grunnett played in Peoples Temple, one has to question this assumption. Certainly for Vernon Gosney and Monica Bagby, the Temple failed them; working in the fields was unfulfilling, and both felt that the dream and promise of Jonestown had turned into a lie. Indeed, Temple member Larry Layton, who shot Vernon and Monica, expressed remorse at shooting him because many Jonestown residents often ridiculed him for being too flamboyant. It is no wonder that Vernon who, in addition to the other indignities of Jonestown, was pulled from the pageant show and picked on, would want to leave the community. Jonestown did not live up to its promise to him. He did not reject Jonestown, but rather, in a sense, Jonestown rejected him.

Maybe the Temple failed Vernon and Monica while allowing Pat, Loretta and Deanna the space to grow and explore their lives. Peoples Temple could do both things. However, given the demise of the community, one wonders if the Jonestown experience could have been anything but failure for all of the Temple members. As Vernon points out, "Hundreds of people were suffering in silence. The dream we shared was a shattered nightmare. Our leader was a despot. How could anyone deem Peoples Temple or Jonestown a success when the people are all dead?"

Certainly gay and lesbian researchers should lead the way in remembering and memorializing a group of people who collectively identified as gay and lesbian. It is clear the gay and lesbian community of San Francisco welcomed Peoples Temple support in opposing the anti-gay ballot initiatives of the late seventies, and that Harvey Milk and Peoples Temple had a mutually supportive and warm relationship right up until November 1978. As more people come forward with their stories, the overall picture of Jonestown, Peoples Temple and Harvey Milk will be made more complete.

This project begins to address the roles of gays and lesbians in this unique American experience. Though many people may not see the need or connections for gay specific research, gays and lesbians are often ignored in history, and are rarely the target audience of stories, by them or about them during contemporary events. We need to explore the relationship between Vernon Gosney and Monica Bagby: what motivated them to leave Jonestown; what impact did that have on other defectors; what role did their homosexuality play in their decision to leave, if it played a role at all? Did the fact that Loretta and Deanna were committed to each other impact their decision to stay in Jonestown? After living openly in Jonestown, was there despair at the thought of returning to a homophobic, anti-gay American society?

If we do not focus on the fact that these people were gay and lesbian, then the general perception is that they were straight. Though that is not terrible, their gayness is part of who they were and what they did, and therefore it should be mentioned, and, where relevant, should be explored. Certainly if gay and lesbian researchers do not embark into this new field of research, gay and lesbian stories will be lost to time. It has been 30 years, and this is the first work to consider the gay experiences of Peoples Temple. This is not a criticism of straight researchers; rather it is a call for queer-sensitive researchers to take the time and explore the gayness of history, regardless of whether or not the subject is deemed a "gay issue."

$\mathcal{W}$HERE ARE THEY TODAY?

Monica Bagby was the only person wounded on the airstrip that the Guyanese pilots felt comfortable to fly out on November 18, probably because she was black. She lost a part of her lung, and the doctors were not able to remove all of the shrapnel from her body. Upon entering the country, she told the FBI that she did not feel safe returning home as she thought that her mother would not forgive her for leaving Jonestown, for not committing suicide with the rest of the group. She moved in with Linda Mertle and maintained ties with Vernon Gosney for years. She moved to southern California.

Vernon Gosney took time adjusting to life after Jonestown, recovering from his life-threatening wounds and the tragic loss of his son. He stayed in the Bay Area for a while, reconnecting with Jamie Gill and hanging out. He repaired his relationship with his family and eventually moved to Hawaii where he joined law enforcement. In 2001 he surprised many people by appearing at Larry Layton's parole hearing with powerful testimony resulting in Larry's release.

Garry Lambrev was devastated at the news of Jonestown. He moved around for a while but eventually settled back in the Bay Area. He still lives in the Berkeley area, and helps network with former Temple members and Jonestown survivors.

Alan Swanson stayed in the Ukiah area where he lives today. He and Garry Lambrev remained good friends throughout the years.

Linda Mertle lives in the Bay Area. Her father and step-mother, Al and Jeanne Mills, were killed in their Berkeley home in what is still an unsolved murder. Linda also networks with former Temple members, Jonestown survivors and family members.

$\mathcal{N}$OTES ON SOURCES

A number of people were very helpful, spending hours during interviews to form this document. Former Temple members Vernon Gosney and Laura Johnston Kohl gave limitless guidance and were very open about their experiences in Jonestown. Garry Lambrev, Linda Mertle and Alan Swanson spent hours reviewing their involvement in Peoples Temple. Rebecca Moore, PhD and her husband Fielding McGehee via their Internet website (*http:// jonestown.sdsu.edu/*) answered multitudes of requests. Their transcribing of numerous tapes kept by Peoples Temple is invaluable to researchers.

Daniel Nicolletta opened his home to me and was the first associate of Harvey Milk to give insight into the relationship between Milk and Jim Jones.

In addition to information supplied by Vernon Gosney, notes about Monica Bagby's interaction with Keith Wade came from her FBI interview, as well as her deposition for the wrongful injury lawsuit against the Temple.

Jeannie Mills and her husband, Al, reconstructed conversations in *Six Years with God* from memory, changing the names of Temple members they wrote about, the incidents may be reliable, the names are not. There was a concern of relying too heavily on the Mills' accounts, as their relationship with the Temple was so hostile, and they use homosexuality as an example of depravity within the Temple. However survivors did recall her stories, and often knew whom the stories were about despite the pseudonyms, so they were considered reliable and included.

The biographies of Peoples Temple members who died in Jonestown were reconstructed from their Temple membership records, recollections of surviving members specifically Linda Mertle, Laura Kohl Johnston and Vernon Gosney, as well as the books *Raven* by Tim Reiterman and John Jacobs, and *The Strongest Poison* by Mark Lane.

A large amount of research was done at the California Historical Society, which houses the papers from Peoples Temple when it was closed in 1979, as well as the documents from the receivership and liquidation of the Temple. Located at 678 Mission Street in San Francisco, the North Baker Research Library is open Wednesday through Friday from noon to 5:00 pm. Admission is free, although the staff appreciates advance notice of the arrival of researchers; call 415-357-1848.

Harvey Milk's papers are located at the San Francisco Public Library, Sixth Floor reading room, 100 Larkin Street (at Grove) in San Francisco. Hours vary during the week; call 415-557-4400 for details. Also housed at the San Francisco Library are the papers of Milk biographer Randy Shilts. These were very helpful in that a number of people interviewed by Shilts – and Shilts himself – are no longer alive. However, because the interviews were done after the Jonestown tragedy, they lack the same clarity and insight they would have if they had been taken earlier.

$\mathcal{W}$ORKS CITED

Feinsod, Ethan. *Awake in a Nightmare. Jonestown: The Only Eyewitness Account*. New York: W. W. Norton, 1981.

Hall, John R., *Gone from the Promised Land: Jonestown in American Cultural History*. New Brunswick, N.J.: Transaction Publishers, 1987; reprint 2004.

Jones, Cleve and Jeff Dawson, *Stitching a Revolution: The Making of an Activist*. San Francisco: Harper San Francisco, 2001.

Kahalas, Laurie Efrein, *Snake Dance: Unraveling the Mysteries of Jonestown*. New York: Red Robin Press, 1998.

Kilduff, Marshall and Ron Javers. *The Suicide Cult: The Inside Story of the Peoples Temple Sect and the Massacre in Guyana*. New York: Bantam, 1978.

Klineman, George and Sherman Butler, and David Conn. *The Cult that Died: the Tragedy of Jim Jones and the People's Temple*. New York: G. P. Putnam's Sons, 1980.

Krause, Charles, with Laurence M. Stern, Richard Harwood and the staff of the *Washington Post. Guyana Massacre: The Eyewitness Account*. New York: Berkley Publishing, 1978.

Landau, Nathan. *Heavenly Deceptor*. Brooklyn, N.Y.: Sound of Music Publishing, 1992.

Lane, Mark. *The Strongest Poison*. New York: Hawthorn Books, 1980.

Maaga, Mary McCormick. *Hearing the Voices of Jonestown*. Syracuse, N.Y.: Syracuse University Press, 1998.

Maguire, John and Mary Lee Dunn. *Hold Hands and Die*. New York: Dale, 1978.

Meiers, Michael. *Was Jonestown a CIA Medical Experiment?: A Review of the Evidence*. Lewiston, N.Y.: The Edwin Mellen Press, 1988.

Mills, Jeannie. *Six Years with God: Life inside Rev. Jim Jones's Peoples Temple*. New York: A&W Publishers, 1979.

Moore, Rebecca, Anthony B. Pinn, and Mary R. Sawyer, eds. *Peoples Temple and Black Religion in America*. Bloomington and Indianapolis: University of Indiana Press, 2004.

Naipaul, Shiva. *Journey to Nowhere: A New World Tragedy*. New York: Penguin Books, 1980.

Nugent, John Peer. *White Night: The Untold Story of What Happened Before— and Beyond—Jonestown*. New York: Rawson, Wade Publishers, 1979.

Reiterman, Tim, with John Jacobs. *Raven: The Untold Story of the Rev. Jim Jones and His People*. New York: E. P. Dutton, 1982.

Shilts, Randy, *The Mayor of Castro Street: The Life and Times of Harvey Milk*. New York: St. Martin's Press, 1982.

Weightman, Judith. *Making Sense of the Jonestown Suicides*. Lewiston, N.Y.: The Edwin Mellen Press, 1983.

Weiss, Mike, *Double Play: The San Francisco City Hall Killings*. Reading, MA: Addison-Wesley Publishing Co., 1984.

White, Mel. *Deceived*, Old Tappan, N.J.: Spire Books, 1979.

Newspapers

Bay Area Reporter

The Black Panther

The New York Times

San Francisco Chronicle

San Francisco Examiner

San Francisco Sentinel

The Sun Reporter

Other resources

Alternative Considerations of Jonestown and Peoples Temple,
   http://jonestown.sdsu.edu/

Peoples Temple Collection, California Historical Society, MS 3800 ff

FBI Bu-File 89-4286, RYMUR [Ryan Murder] and Jonestown

San Francisco Public Library, Randy Shilts Collection

www.ingramcontent.com/pod-product-compliance
Lightning Source LLC
Chambersburg PA
CBHW020255290526
45784CB00003B/1257